M000316732

PENETRATION

Sheena E.

The following is based on true events. Names, dates, locations, and other facts have been changed to protect the privacy of those involved.

Penetration:

1.

The action or process of making a way through or into something.

2.

The perceptive understanding of complex matters.

Atlantic City, New Jersey, 2004

Tropicana always had a way better band playing then Bally's or Caesars. I had the nerve to have adapted a preference. One of my closest male friends, let's call him Mr. C, had introduced me to "the life" a few months ago, and I agreed to be his eyes and ears since the security guards and undercover law enforcement knew how to spot a pimp a mile away. This was like my second month of what I like to call "babysitting the hos." I used to think a bitch would have to be out of her mind to be a ho and have a pimp, but since I had been around C and his girls I'd grown a certain amount of respect for these chicks. They were more than just some simpleminded females having sex for money and giving it to men... in fact they hardly ever had sex.

This one ho named Joy, she was the baddest chick he had. They called her type the bottom bitch. She was there the longest and could get away with a lot more than the other girls. She was a small-framed, half-white, half-Rican chick about 5'2" with thick dark hair. Her body wasn't really much to talk about. She had small, perky breasts and a tight little behind. The men liked her because she had these deep, dark eyes—when she looked at you she captivated you. She had some serious game too. She had these tricks thinking she really cared about them. She had a bunch of regulars too. Men that would escape once or twice a month to AC to spend time with her. She pulled a decent amount of money every night.

Joy taught me how to get paid for conversation. She would sit down seduce me with her eyes and teach me how she got the trick to open up to her. They would tell her a bunch of stories. She would laugh and get paid. Sex or not, they would be so happy to have a beautiful woman sitting next to them. They would never complain. I watched her get close to a hundred grand from a trick she never even fucked. Crazy, right? I know it sounds like a buncha bullshit, but it's the truth.

Six months in and Joy had taught me so much. It was getting so hard to live my regular life. I wasn't looking at men the same since I had started going over to Atlantic City. I was starting to understand how important it was for a man to give me money; being around all the girls and watching how easy it was for them to make money was starting to feel so tempting. I could never work, I was tripping my mother would kill me! What the hell was I thinking? I did know someone that would be down to make some money though. My girlfriend Nia.

Nia and I had become really good friends over the past year. We used to see each other out at the club a lot. I always admired the way she wore sex on her face. I had never met a woman that walked around with so much sexual confidence. Nia was about my height at 5'8"-5'9", brown sugar complexion, with these big-ass tits and wide-ass hips. She was a brick house way before females were getting their bodies altered surgically. Her ass sat up like a professional dancer. Her body was an automatic man magnet. She was built, but her face was really average. She had a slightly widened nose and these thin lips. She always wore this pale pink lipstick from Mac called pink poodle, which made her lips appear bigger and fuller than they were. We saw each other at a party one night. I had been watching her the entire night, just controlling the room. I became a little envious of how much male attention she was getting, but before I could allow my jealousy to kick in I decided I was going to have to make her my friend. I walked over to the bathroom as she was coming out, and we finally exchanged numbers.

The first time we linked up I caught a cab down North Philly to her apartment. We were both from west Philly but her family owned this apartment down north and that's where she lived by herself. I was hyped to see how she was living. I couldn't wait to get there. Nia's apartment wasn't in the best area, but she had it decorated like a page in *Vogue* magazine. I walked in and was greeted by all white and pale pink furniture. She had a Victorian style living room set up with light blush colored carpet. I asked if she wanted me to take my shoes off when I walked in, and she didn't but I took them off anyway. Her dining set was all glass, there were fresh pink flowers in a vase as the center piece, she had candles lit, and owned the most beautiful drapes I had ever seen. She didn't have a TV or anything, just the latest fashion magazines scattered around and a radio. She had a Jadakiss CD playing when I got there.

We immediately started talking about men. She was telling me about her guys she had: some married some not, some she just used for sex, and others were just around to pass her off money when she needed it. I had a few players too, but I had ever been one to kiss and tell. Plus I wanted her to always feel like she was teaching me something. I wasn't a good girl by far, and it always surprised me when people would tell me who they thought I was before we actually got to know each other. I wasn't at all a sucker for love. I had been through my share of stuff with men. I had learned a long time ago not to be so trusting of a man. We found out that we had a lot in common. We laughed and talked all night long and planned to make our first appearance together at the next big party. We quickly became double trouble. She was the sexy one and I was the classier one just by the way we dressed, though we both had game and knew how to use it.

We would start our week off by counting all our money, and most weeks we would start with about five hundred all together. We would deduct our weekly maintenance from that amount to see what we had left over. Maintenance included us both having our nails done and our brows and lashes. Nia had since turned me on to this black-owned spa where they would tint and arch our brows and apply individual lash extensions to our eyelashes. We were spending well over 200 dollars a piece on that alone. So that meant we needed to recoup all the money we spent from men. And most weeks we did that plus more. Nia was also a waitress in this all-white diner, and she made a lot of money in tips. So she always had cash around. I was still doing my hair and makeup jobs, plus I had a few loyal sponsors so money was never hard to come by for us. We got really close, really fast, and we had a tight bond and common interest... get money!

I had mentioned Mr. C to her a few times, so when I asked her to take the ride with me over AC she was on board with it. I told her to wear her uniform, which was tight jeans and a crisp white button down shirt. She always unbuttoned at least the first four buttons, showing off her huge breasts. On the ride down from Philly I was preparing her for what she was about to see. We had been to the casinos on normal terms, like just hanging out or attending fights. But going on a mission was totally different. You had to pay attention to every single person in the building, when you talked to men you had to use your words wisely and never actually mention that you were selling yourself. You had better not say a word about sex for money. There were undercovers posing as regular guys scattered throughout every casino, they were called "vice". They would be on the floor playing different games, even at the slot machines. It was their jobs to blend in and seem normal. I also had to school her to the pimps. It was so hard for me to believe that there were real pimps in Atlantic City. I only ever saw them on HBO and old movies from the 70s, but pimps were real and once I stepped into "the life," I was learning firsthand how dangerous they were. I had to let Nia know what they looked like. They weren't walking around in bright suits; they were wearing jeans and tee shirts just like regular dudes. The permed hair and long curls was a thing of the past. Today's pimps wore short haircuts and had beards just like the guys we dated back home. It was easy to confuse them for normal guys. The most important thing I had to teach her was how to walk pass one. In the pimp game if a ho made eye contact with another pimp she had to go with him. It was like making eye contact was code for I want to work for you. And the more experienced the pimp was the more he lived by this rule. I always had a problem with the whole pimp and ho game so I made it clear to Mr. C from day one that he had to get word to the other pimps that I wasn't working. I was one of them. Nia seemed to understand how important the no eye contact rule was, but she thought it was a joke. I was sure praying we didn't have any issues with the other pimps because I didn't even tell C that I was coming down, so I didn't really have any protection.

Once you step into the door, the whole building looks different. For me, everybody looked like a cop. Anybody that made eye contact with me was suspect. We started at Caesars, we walked in and decided to walk the floor. We glanced over at the blackjack tables just to see what type of men were in the building. We ended up at the bar, I ordered us some wine, and we just sat around talking for a while. About an hour into the conversation this older white man made eye contact with both of us. I gestured for him to approach, and he came over. He was so nervous. I could tell he had never sat down between two black women, and he introduced himself fumbling over his words. The more he talked, the more red his face became. He wasn't sure if we were working, but he was definitely letting us know he was a trick. Nia was good at seduction, so it didn't take her long to get his number, and she also gave him hers. We never actually stated our intentions, but in the life, you don't really have to. Tricks knew without you saying. The action was pretty slow at Caesars, so we left and decided to go to Tropicana.

The bar at Tropicana was always action packed. We sat in front of the stage where this live band was playing. It was key for us to blend in and seem to be just two regular girls having a night out. The vice (undercover cops) were usual making their rounds in this bar. We enjoyed some drinks and conversation, and all of a sudden her phone rang. It was Mr. Fumbles we met earlier. He was inviting Nia to his room, he said he was staying at Bally's, and just wanted to "talk." She was cool with it, and I didn't need to babysit her, so she got up and left. I told her to text me the room info and meet me back at this bar as soon as she was done. This was Nia's first trick.

I immediately started to feel bad. I mean I had my best friend selling herself to a strange man in Atlantic City. Did this make me a pimp? I didn't know how I was going to pass the time, and all I could think about was what she was up there doing. It's funny I never thought about Mr. C's girls. I just did my job, dropped them off and picked them up. I was just the eyes in that situation. But now I felt so responsible for her safety. We talked about our plan to take over the city for weeks before we came out here, but now I was starting to have second thoughts. I had allowed the thought of making a lot of money cloud my better judgement. It was too late now, though. She was upstairs and was officially a prostitute.

Finally Nia came back, and I wanted to know every detail about her first encounter. I could tell she didn't want to tell me, so I didn't ask. We ended our night right after she got back, never really talking about the details of her first date. I dropped her off home, she handed me $300, and said she would call me tomorrow.

The next day we went back, and soon about two months had past. Nia and I had a weekly routine. We would drive over to AC at least twice a week. She was making crazy money and even had a few regulars. She said it was so much easier to deal with the tricks in AC; they were nothing like the niggas back home. Getting money from regular guys was always a game. You have to make up stores and even pretend to be their girlfriends before they would pass off stacks of money. But

AC was different. It was like taking candy from a baby. These men came with the intent to spend some money, and the best part was if you were smart you never had to sleep with them. I started to look forward to our weekly trips as well. I wasn't doing anything but driving, and Nia was breaking me off at least $500 dollars a night, so if we went twice, I was making at least a thousand dollars, and I was cool with that.

So one night as I'm doing my usual, just waiting for Nia and enjoying my forth glass of wine. This young black guy comes and sits at the bar next to me. I could tell he was upset about something, so I asked if he was okay. He started to tell me about all this money he just lost playing craps and how he needed to get some of his losses back. I convinced him to play some more, and he invited me to join him. We walked over to the crap table and he laid out 20 one hundred dollar bills across the table. The dealer counted it and gave him that amount in chips. He began to place his bets and right away he started winning. Every time he hit, he would hand me chips. He was moving so fast I didn't even get a chance to see the amount each chip was worth. He was ordering rum and coke left and right. The more he drank, the more chips he handed me.

I wasn't even thinking about him as a trick in the beginning, but by now I had to at least have a thousand dollars of his money in my bag. I had to think of something fast. For the next few rounds I started to get a little closer to him. I moved my seat close and started to rub his leg as he played. Every time he looked at me I licked my lips at him. I wanted him to believe I was turned on by him even though in reality I would have never looked twice at this guy. He was about six feet tall, super thin, and he had this goofy hair cut with a part. He was obviously not my type, but the stacks of chips in my pocketbook was enough motivation for me to do what I had to do. I started ordering rum and coke just like him. I wasn't drinking mine, though. I would sit it on the rim on the other side of the crap table and pretend I was drinking just as much as he was. He continued to win and pass me chips for at least another forty minutes before I started to act like I had to pee. I was wobbling in my seat all the while rubbing his leg, sometimes even allowing my hand to get close to his penis. Finally I whispered to him that I needed to use the restroom. He didn't put up a fight, and he didn't ask me for his chips back. I grabbed my bag and walked quickly away from the crap table peaking back to see if he was paying me any attention. He wasn't, so I looked up and located the nearest cash-in booth. I ran to the cash-in and emptied all the chips on the counter. The man looked at me and smiled, "Got lucky tonight, huh?" he giggled, and I just smiled. He handed me over $1,760 dollars, cash.

I thought about going back over to the guy, but then I thought about who I was. I wasn't a regular girl looking for a new friend. I was working, and I had just scored my first trick. I rushed out the doors of the casino and ran to my car. I couldn't wait to pull off. I texted Nia to meet me over at the Borgata, one of the newer casinos a few miles away from Caesars, so even if he went to look for me he would never find me. I never told Nia about my score that night. I don't even have a reason, I just never mentioned it. But when she offered me a cut of her money I declined. I wasn't going to be greedy; plus I knew she worked way harder for her money than I did.

The next few trips we made, I refused to go in Caesars. I wasn't sure if the guy had reported me. For all I knew they had my picture plastered on the walls, so I told Nia we should start working over at the Borgata. I convinced her that since it was a newer casino, there had to be a bigger score in the building. She agreed.

The Borgata was a whole new playing field. C had never sent his girls over here, and I didn't see any of the local pimps walking through the casino either. Unlike the other casinos Borgata was beautiful. Everything was brand new. When you walked in, you were greeted by fans blowing fresh, crisp, clean air instead of the usual stench of cigarette smoke. Even the floors shined like new money. I loved the Borgata. I had been there a few times on dates and even came to see Alicia Keys perform there once. It was the closest thing to Las Vegas that Atlantic City had to offer. Since I had never "worked" the Borgata, I wanted to take things really slow. I needed to come and people watch a few times to get a feel for how things worked around there. Unlike the older casinos, Borgata didn't have a large bar area. It was modern, so it actually had full nightclubs inside the casino. The bar area was much smaller. That meant it offered less room to blend in, so we had to come up with a plan in order to not look suspicious.

Nia didn't like the Borgata as much as me. She was already used to the raw, gritty side of working that she experienced over on the other side of town. I was over it; the Borgata was my type of place. I felt more like myself over there. I wanted to make it work, but Nia was rejecting every suggestion I made. I thought it would be a good idea for Nia to change up her look when we worked over here, as her porn star white collar shirt was dead giveaway, and she needed to appear to be a little more sophisticated to appeal to the high rollers throughout the building. In order to score big on this side of town we had to play the game a brand new way. These weren't just old men looking for some conversation. These were CEOs and businessmen looking to have their sexual fantasies play out in front of them. I could tell we could make a lot more money, but it was going to take a lot more than lip licking and unbuttoned shirts. Nia was so resistant to the new way I wanted to work, so one night I decided to take the ride over by myself.

I arrived at the Borgata about 11pm. My plan was to play on some slots, visit the bar, and just see how things went over here. Yeah, I didn't notice anybody working, but this was still Atlantic City, so I knew there had to be some girls in there. They were just doing a good job of blending. I decided to sit at the bar and have a glass of wine to start my night off.

Three glasses later, and I sorta forgot what I'm there for. I was grooving to the music and having conversations with myself in my head. All of a sudden this older white gentleman sat next to me. At first he didn't say anything, but I could feel him staring at me, so I looked up, stared right into his eyes and said, "Hello."

He greeted me, and asked what I'm drinking. I notice he's having some type of mixed drink, so I said, "I'm having whatever it is you're drinking." That broke the ice. He laughed and ordered another round. Ten minutes passed, and we were talking about nonsense. I can tell he wasn't expecting to have anything in common with me, but we both were Celtic fans, and we spent a good while talking about the recent trades and a whole bunch of basketball stuff. He was an older man with a little patch of grey in the front of his head, had a medium build and was tall, at least 6'3". He told me he owned a yacht design company and they were in town for some type of convention. He gave me his business card and asked how long I was in town, so I told him I was finishing up a long week in the city and was headed back in the morning. This was a lie, but he didn't need to know the truth. He asked if he could have my number. I didn't decline, and he left. I sat here enjoying the last of my mystery drink.

My stakeout went on for about another hour when I decided it was time to take the ride back over the bridge. I was a little tipsy but not drunk. I knew my limit when it came to liquor. I never wanted to drive back home drunk; my mom would kill me if I crashed her car, plus she didn't even know I was driving back and forth to Atlantic City a few nights a week. So I headed down the escalator to the valet to get the car when I felt my phone vibrate. I see an unknown number come across the screen, and I immediately knew it was the Mystery Drink from the bar.

I answered and he asked me if I wouldn't mind coming to his room. He said he just wanted to continue the conversation we were having at the bar. Code words for "I'm a trick and I want to pay you for some time." I went back and forth in my head about it before I finally said yes. I couldn't believe I agreed to go up to his room. This wasn't a role I was comfortable playing. I wasn't a ho. I was just here to make sure things went smooth for the other girls. *Shit, what did I just agree to?* As I rode the elevator up to his room it felt like everybody was watching me. It was like I had the words "ho" written on my forehead. All I could think about was it being a setup, maybe the people from Caesars setting me up because I stole that money a few weeks ago. My heart was pounding, but in typical fashion, I ignored the funny feeling I was having and knocked on his door. He called for me to come inside. I had never been on the inside of a room at the Borgata. It was beautiful, the drapes hit the floor, and the furniture was sleek and sexy. As I walked in I noticed he was nowhere to be found, I didn't even know his name, so I couldn't call out for him. I just stood there for a minute before I heard his voice coming form the next room.

"I'm in here," he said in a muffled voice. I walked into the next room and there he is butt naked in a tub full of bubbles. I really just wanted to run out of there, but I was there already and I secretly wanted to see how this was going to play out. He asked if he could see my breasts. I was shocked. He had all of a sudden became very demanding. I asked him how bad he wanted to see them, and he said, "How about $500 dollars bad?" I laughed and said he couldn't see my bra for $500 dollars, so he asked what about $700 dollars, so I said he could see one of them for the $700. I could tell he was enjoying this game of back and forth, and he told me to grab his wallet and take out the cash and count it. I counted $4,700 dollars. He told me take out $1,400 because he wanted to see both breasts, so I proceeded to take off my shirt and bra. I stood in front of him, and with no shame exposed my full 36 D breasts. His white face lit up like a kid on Christmas morning. Deep down inside I was starting to enjoy the control he was allowing me to have. I walked over to the tub and leaned my breasts in his

face, teasing him as I let my nipples bounce on his forehead.
I could tell he was getting excited. I also knew that he a lot
more money to spend, and at this point I was trying to cash
out. I teased him for a few more minutes then I walked back
to grab my shirt, and just as I thought, he begged me not to
put it back on. He wanted me to get inside the tub with him. I
wasn't about to sit in no dirty tub water with a white man, so
I told him he could get out and I would refill it and get inside
by myself. He wanted to play he said, so I told him he could
watch me play, that I liked to play alone. He was so excited
and already hypnotized by the sight of my perky tits, so he
agreed. Watching this middle aged white man get out of the
tub is one sight I will never forget. His ass sagged a little, but
he surprisingly had a pretty nice body. I wasn't about to fall in
love with this man, and I pretended not to even notice. Once
the tub was cleaned and refilled, he brought a chair into the
room and sat it right next to the tub. As I got in I gestured for
him to give me more cash, so he placed another $300 dollars
in my hand as I sat in the water. My plan was to play with my
breasts for a while and eventually fake an orgasm.

But Mystery Drink had other plans. He wanted to ejaculate
on my breasts. He literally pleaded with me to allow him to.
By now something had triggered inside my head. I wanted
to make him work for it. I wasn't even thinking about the
money at this point. I had realized that I had some type of
control over this man. I knew that I could pretty much get
him to do whatever I wanted him to do, and I had to test
out my new skills. So I told him to stand up and take his
underwear off. I wanted to watch him get his penis hard. He
didn't waste a single minute. He took his underwear down
and began to stroke his penis. He was stroking it too slow, so I
demanded that he stroke it faster. The faster he stroked it, the
harder it became. I could tell by his eyes that he was about to
reach his peak. I leaned my body half way out of the tub and
allowed my breasts to sit on the edge. I grabbed both his legs,
pulling him closer to me and his penis burst on to my breasts.
The warm, thick semen gave me an instant rush. I watched

as his eyes rolled back in his head and he sat back down in his chair. I didn't say a word. I wiped his liquid off my chest, dried my body off, put my clothes back on, and walked out the door. My mind was racing and my body was oozing with pure satisfaction. I couldn't control my own fluids, and as I approached the elevator, I felt a rush of cream flow out of my pussy. I was so turned on. It wasn't about the money. I was now addicted to the power. So much was going through my mind. I had never experienced anything like it. And I couldn't wait to feel like that again.

I saw Mystery Drink a few more times after our first encounter, and each time he would allow me to control him sexually. Before meeting him, I was a little aggressive. I would be the one to initiate sex in most of my SituationShips. I call them SituationShips because I had never been in a serious relationship. Most of the guys I dealt with were either somebody else's man or guys I was "with" but we never gave it a title. I had become very comfortable being the more aggressive one in mostly all my encounters. If I was out and saw someone I wanted, I would approach him and get his number. I was always bold and very upfront. After dealing with those tricks in Atlantic City, I discovered how I could transform my aggressiveness into control. Mystery Drink would let me call all the shots. I would tell him to get naked when I walked into the hotel room, and he would listen. I would walk into the room wearing this long leather coat with nothing but a bra and tank top under it and my clear platform heels. I would immediately restrict his hands and feet, and I would also place a few ice cubes down the front of his underwear. Mystery Drink had a cold fetish—he loved for his penis and nipples to be numb. I had grown to love his reaction to the gradual numbing of his body parts. His pale face would tense up, and he would let out these pathetic moans. Hearing his cries quickly became one of my favorite parts of our meet ups. I enjoyed standing over him, wearing my six-inch heels, pressing the heel of the shoe into his flesh occasionally just to see him turn red. I would do a little strip tease, taking my jacket off first, covering his face with it, sliding it off, and throwing it back in his face. Next I would take off my tank top, slapping him in his face a few times, making him beg for me to take off my bra and allow him to see my beautiful breasts that he fell in love with months earlier when we first met.

My breasts were the star of every show. I would make him open his mouth really wide and tease his top lip with my nipples. His mouth would start to water at the sight of my erect pink nipples. I would allow him to gently suck on my nipples before I took them away from him. His request was always the same: he wanted to cum on my breasts. I would untie his hands and he would stroke himself until he was ready to climax, and like clockwork he would explode onto my D cups. Every time I would clean myself off, get dressed, and walk out the door. Mystery Drink and I had eventually got to the point where we would make cash deposits onto my prepaid debt card, so making my exit had become much smoother. My body reacted the same after every encounter. I would approach the elevator and by the time I got to my car, my pussy would have already dripped down my bare legs. I was experiencing extreme pleasure. I had allowed myself to reach my sexual peak without having a man enter inside me.

Mystery Drink became a thing of the past after about nine months of us dealing with each other. Maybe he all of a sudden felt guilty for his behavior, or maybe he had found himself another girl to help him play. I walked away from that situation with a newfound confidence, and I was able to make thousands of dollars without adding a body to my list of sexual partners. Either way you look at it, I was the winner.

A couple of months had passed since Mystery Drink and I lost contact. I can't front like I wasn't a little salty; I was even a little mad. I had become so depended on that extra money that not having him anymore was starting to become a problem for my growing shopping habit. Mr. C had also decided to take his operation on the road, so him and his girls went over to Las Vegas. You never realize how much money you really spend until you don't have any. I wasn't looking forward to getting back in touch with any of my old playas. I was preparing myself to get back to hustling street niggaz, making up sob stories, and faking pregnancies for abortion money. All the stuff I thought I would never have to do again. I could either go back to that, or take the ride over to AC and find a new victim.

My prayers were answered pretty quickly when I got a phone call from one of my girlfriends about some random guy that just had to meet me. He had saw me and her out together a few times and wanted to know if he could take me on a date. Now I wouldn't normally agree, because since my AC run I wasn't really feeling "street guys," but I was banking on him being a check provider, so I decided to take him up on the date offer.

Two days later

I arrived at Wizards a little before 10pm. Wizards is a low-key strip club in west Philly. It's a little below my standards, but I never pass up chance to look at females with better bodies than mine. I think my date; we will call him "Checks," was a little surprised when I insisted he meet me here. I know not too many females want to hang out in the strip club, but I loved it. Every time I met guys in the strip club, I was able to see his true colors within minutes. It's really hard to hide your sexual side in a room full of half-naked women. Plus I needed to see what kind of tipper he was. Usually if a guy threw money to the strippers he was stingy. A show off will get a ton of one dollar bills and make it rain on the girls, causing a scene and pretending like money isn't a thing. I've seen that one too many times. I admired the type of guy that let me hold the money, giving me full control of the money and allowing me to pick the girls I wanted to tip. That's the type of guys I like.

I waited for him upstairs at the cheesesteak shop right above the strip club. Wizards didn't allow females in unless they were with a man. Finally he walked in wearing a white tee-shirt and jeans, the "Philly guy" uniform. I can't front; he was a little cutie, a little light for my usual type, but he was cute. He had nice full lips and a sharp low haircut. I really was feeling his footwear; he had on some all leather Chuck Taylors. They were my favorite chill shoe for a man. I stood up at his arrival and he gave me a light hug. I was wearing a tank top and some skinny jeans, my hair pulled back into a French braid.

We walked downstairs into the club and walked to the bar. Checks was pretty quiet at first. I'm sure he was a little nervous because he damn near spilled my drink on me as he handed it to me. The first twenty minutes was rough. He didn't say too much, and he needed to loosen up quick or this date was about to be over. I asked him if he took shots, and when he said no, I ordered two double shots of Grey Goose anyway. Four rounds later, and he's finally coming around, so I got the attention of the baddest strippers in the whole club and I let him have his way with them. He let me hold the money too. The night was going pretty well. We didn't talk about much, but I found out we both loved basketball and boxing, so that was a start. A couple hours later he's totally wasted and asked me if I would come to his house. I agreed.

I wasn't planning to have sex with him, but I didn't want him to get a DUI driving back to his place. I moved my car out of the metered parking space and got inside his. He lived in this suburban part of the city called Conshohocken. We arrived at his complex, and I have to admit I was a little impressed at how his place was laid out. As soon as we walked in, he went straight to the bathroom to shower. I walked around checking out his furniture. He had they typical bachelor pad stuff, like a big screen TV and a leather sofa set. But he had a vintage record player over in the corner and his walls were filled with old record covers in frames. Being a lover of music, I was really feeling the décor.

He got out of the shower and walked into the living room wearing nothing but a towel. He walked over to me and took his index finger and ran it across my top lip. "What's up with those?" he asked as his finger glided back and forth along my lip.

"What does that mean?" I asked... Of course, I knew full well what he wanted. That was code for suck my dick. I was hip but still playing naïve.

Either it was the Grey Goose or I was just craving a dick in my mouth, but either way he was standing over me seconds later, feeding his dick to me like food. Checks actually had a very nice dick. It was thick and long, had a slight curve to it. It fit perfectly into my mouth, which gave me the ability to really go to work. I allowed his balls to swim inside the pools of saliva in my mouth as I stroked his dick with my hands. It didn't take long before my jeans were being unbuttoned and my pussy was exposed. He pushed my body back against the loveseat and spread my legs wide open. His mouth felt so good my pussy lips; he must have washed his mouth out with some mouthwash when he showered because I was getting this tingling feeling as he licked. He was doing a pretty good job at sucking my clit, but it had been so long since I actually had intercourse I was ready to feel him inside me. He slid a condom on and held my one leg back really far with his right arm, forced his curvy manhood inside me, and a few strokes in he was ready to cum. I couldn't believe it! We had only been at it for about seven minutes when he let out the loudest grunt and shot his load into the condom. I can't front I was a little disappointed in his performance. I wasn't even able to cum. He rolled over and asked me to get him a warm rag from the bathroom. I went inside the bathroom, had to pee, and then I grabbed a rag for him to wash off with. As I approached him on the sofa, he asked me to grab a Gucci shopping bag from the bedroom closet. Thinking nothing of it, I grabbed it for him. As I made my way back in to the living room I noticed he was now sitting straight up in his seat. He asked if I looked into the bag. "No," I replied as he took it out of my hands. He gave me this creepy smirk and asked me to sit next to him. So I did. Checks opened the shopping back and pulled out a double sided dildo. I couldn't believe my eyes. I was thinking, *What the fuck does he want to do with that?*

"You ever used one of these?" he asked.

"No," I lied. I had used sex toys in the past. I just wasn't sure what his plans were, and I wasn't about to seem like an expert. Plus, the dildo had to be a good fifteen inches, so I wasn't about to let him kill me with no fake dick.

"You like anal?" Checks was starting to worry me.

I told him I had done it a few times in the past with my ex, but I wasn't a fan. Again, this was a lie. Anal was actually one of my favorite positions. True I had done it for the first time a few years ago, but there was never a better feeling of pleasure than a firm dick forced into your asshole.

"I'm not talking about getting your ass fucked. I'm talking about fucking somebody's ass."

"What"? I asked in a low tone.

"Just what I said, how do you feel about fucking somebody in the ass?"

"I mean, I guess I would do it."

"Well, let's go," the words came out in slow motion. I couldn't believe what I was hearing he wanted me to fuck him in the ass with the double-sided dildo. Now I was no stranger to freak shit, but this was on a whole other level. I thought about it for a few and then decided to just do it. Checks' eyes lit up like a kid on Christmas morning. He got the KY out of the bag and laid on his stomach. He scooted his ass in the air a little and signaled me with his finger to come closer. "Don't be scared," he said in a very demanding tone. I looked down at the dildo, then down at his round, brown ass, swallowed the lump in my throat, and proceeded to drive the dick inside his not so tight asshole.

At first I felt so crazy, but the deeper the dildo reached inside him, the easier it became on my end. He pulled my body closer to his allowing my breast to rest on his back, and he stared, touching his own balls. He threw his body up against me to request more pressure, and suddenly I got lost in the moment. I started pounding his ass with no regard for the amount of pain I could be causing. My body got so warm, I felt like I was in another world as he let out some of the loudest moans I had ever heard come from a man. He was loving every second of it. Oddly, so was I. As his body started to tense up I knew he was about to cum. I eased the dildo out of his asshole, flipped him over, and sucked the nut out of his dick. We both fell on our backs instantly.

So much was going through my mind. I couldn't believe I had just fucked a man, and I think I enjoyed it more than he did. My pussy was dripping uncontrollably. I had so unexpectedly reached a new level of power. We dozed off, and the next day Checks woke up and didn't mention the episode at all. He dropped me back off at my car, handed me a stack of money, and told me he would call me later. I didn't want to count the cash in front of him, so I waited until he pulled off. I peeled back the fifty dollar bills. They added up to $1,800. Not bad.

After that first night, I started seeing Checks on an almost a weekly basis. He would take me out, and we would get drunk. Then I would go back to his apartment and fuck him in the ass. We never had regular sex together. He was so in love with my dick and that's all he wanted. After about the fourth or fifth time he had got so comfortable he would immediately jump in the bed butt naked and get on all fours like he was the female and I was the male. He even stopped eating my pussy. It had become all about his sexual satisfaction. Taking his asshole made me feel like a character from a movie; it was like I was living in a porno. Imagine telling your man to lay down on his back and open his legs wide while you allow your fingers to open up his asshole, preparing it for your fifteen-inch dick to slide inside him. Your man arching his back ready and willing to be pounded by you, making sounds that you never made. Watching his eyes roll back into his head as his dick exploded, and all the while your body's not being touched at all. His sexual confusion became a problem for me after a while. I was blinded by the $2,500 cash he would give me after every session. And there was also this part of me that really enjoyed the feeling of his ass cheeks tightening on the shaft of my dick. I was becoming just as sick as he was. I would lay in the bed beside him and tears would run down my face. I don't know if it was guilt or just my body's way of telling me it was time to leave his ass alone. It was like one day I woke up and just didn't want to be his personal porn star. I was over it. I was over him. Plus I started thinking about all the other women he was fucking and lying to. Did they even know he was gay? Did he have a whole lineup of chicks he paid to stick a dildo up his ass? Checks wasn't happy when I told him I wanted to chill for a little while. I told him some lie about me getting back with an ex-boyfriend. In reality, I didn't want to hurt his feelings. We had got really close, plus I met him through a close friend, I was sure we would see each other again at social events. I had to walk away on good terms.

Yet, my newfound superpower carried over into my other situations as well. I was no longer interested in simple sex. I needed to own a certain amount of power. As much as I hated to admit it, Checks had created a monster. My sexual appetite was starting to take over my life. I wanted to control every encounter. Between Checks and the tricks in AC, I didn't even know who I was anymore. I never wanted to be a prostitute, nor did I ever see myself as a human sex toy. I couldn't understand why I kept putting myself in these intense situations. As much as I wanted to be "normal" and engage in a regular boy meets girl type of relationship, I couldn't shake the world I created for myself.

I started to reflect on some of my very first encounters with men. Was it always just about sex? At almost twenty-five years old, I had yet to experience real love from a man...

Summer 1994

Ant was on his way to come see me. I was so excited. He was one of the cutest guys around the way. Tall, light brown skin, nice full lips. He looked just like Nas the rapper to me. I was so happy my sister took this overnight babysitting job, which meant I could actually spend some time with him. My grandma would never let him come over to our house. I mean, I couldn't really blame her. He was at least twenty. Way too old to be hanging out with us.

Miss Lisa bartended at night. She usually didn't get back until after two in the morning. My sister babysat her son overnight. I went with her to keep her company and have boys over. We had the whole apartment to ourselves all night long. Her son usually went to sleep by ten, and Ant came over almost every night we were there. We usually just sat on the couch and watched TV. He always gave me money before he left. Money and a kiss. This night, something seemed a little different.

I needed to use the bathroom, so I got up and walked down the dark hallway into the bathroom. As I washed my hands, I heard someone turning the door knob. It was Ant.

"Hey, pretty girl." He smiled at me with his arms stretched out for a hug. I hugged him and attempted to walk out of the bathroom.

"Wait," he said as he pushed me up against the wall. "I wanna taste you."

"Taste me?" I asked, totally confused about his words.

"Yeah, taste you. Pull your shorts back down."

As I was pulling my little denim daisy dukes off, he started kissing me on the neck. His mouth felt so cold and wet brushed up against my nervous flesh. I got this strange feeling in the bottom my stomach; he kept kissing me. As my shorts hit the bathroom floor, I felt his hand massaging me through my panties. Ant went to his knees and pulled my panties down with his teeth. Then he started to kiss my box, his lips felt moist. As he started moving his head faster and faster, I began to scream. He stopped, looked me dead in the eyes, and told me to shut up. I listened as he went back down on me. I felt a warm sensation between my legs, and just then he stopped and spun me around so I was facing the bathroom wall. I felt this intense pressure between my legs as he entered my tight hole for the first time. It hurt so bad I wanted to yell and holler, but he was covering my mouth so I wouldn't wake up the sleeping kid. He had his way with me for at least a half hour before he reached his peak onto the rim of the sink, pulled his pants up, and walked out of the bathroom.

I'm not sure if my sister heard me or not, but I didn't mention anything to her about what had just taken place. I sat on the little loveseat next to Ant as he rested his hand on my skinny little thigh. It was after two, and I was getting tired. Ant told me he had to go, and I got up to walk him to the front door. As he walked out, he handed me some cash rolled in a rubber band.

That night it was $450. The amount increased each time we saw each other. He was my first TRICK.

I was 13 years old and I had been paid for sex. I didn't realize it then, but Ant had set the tone for my interaction with men. I had allowed him take my body from me in exchange for hundreds of dollars, a few compliments, and even my first pair of designer shoes. He used to tell me I tasted so good he had to pay me. I was a little girl. I had been manipulated so early. I guess I never had a chance.

West Philly, Summer 2006

My friend Ace was one of the biggest party promoters in the city. We became friends back in the 90s when he and my older cousin went to the same high school. I used to love going up to her school, hanging with the older kids, doing all the stuff they did. I was never really around people my age. Every since I was young I preferred to be around my older family members and friends. I was always taller than most girls my age, and my body was well developed by the time I was in eighth grade, so I was able to blend into the high school crowd long before I was even a freshman.

Ace and I had maintained our friendship over the years. He would let me into his parties for free and even allow me to bring a friend or two. I had made a name for myself in the social scene in Philly. I wasn't the most popular girl, but the right people knew who I was, so I was able to party without paying the cover charge at just about every venue. Ace knew when I called his phone that I wanted him to come outside. He hated that I always waited 'til the last minute to call him about access to his events. He always made sure I got in, and he formed this love/hate type of bond with me. But I knew he cared a lot for me, and he knew I was always a true friend to him as well.

All winter I had worked on my new body image. I took these diet pills and started working out, so I was in the best shape of my life that summer. I was always easy on the eyes, but I had a few extra pounds on my hips and abs that needed to go. I had went from a size 12/14 to a size 8. I had not worn an 8 since high school. Even my breasts had gotten a little smaller; my full D went down to a firm C cup. I was wearing less and showing off my hard work every chance I got. This new body was getting some new attention, and a lot of old faces were all of a sudden missing me so much. It felt good to have all these suitors. I was on a date every night. I never had a problem getting money from guys, but it was like now I didn't even have to ask. I had this one fat guy I would call just to come pay the tab. My girlfriends and I would go out to eat and drink, and he would show up and pay. I was loving everything about this summer. My sex life was at a standstill, though. It seemed like I was more sexually attractive when I was thicker. I was going through my first sexual drought, and I hated it.

Ace hit me up one day and told me he had this friend that wanted to meet me.

"What friend?" I asked. He knew everybody in the city, and I wasn't about to be set up with no cornball. He told me I didn't know this guy at all. His name was... well, let's call him Industry. Industry was a music producer from Philly, but he spent a lot of time in New York, L.A., and Miami. That was all I needed to hear. I was always partial to meeting guys that weren't familiar with who I was publicly. And to hear that he was in the music business was an added bonus. I loved all types of music. I even used to sing when I was younger, so if nothing else, I knew we were sure to connect musically. I allowed Ace to pass my number off to Industry, so when this strange area code popped up on my screen, I knew it was him.

I was immediately turned on by his baritone voice. It felt good to hear the voice of a real man coming through my speaker. He already knew what I looked like because he had saw pictures of me posted on the Nightlife link. Nightlife link was this website that had photographers share pictures from all the parties' throughput the city. Since I was a self-proclaimed socialite, I had a few shots posted monthly. I was never really concerned about Industry's physical appearance. I had stopped caring a lot about what a man looked like on the outside. I didn't need a man thinking he was cuter then me, so as long as I was feeling his overall vibe, I'd give him chance. We planned to meet for the first time at the Continental downtown on Chestnut Street. I was cool with that. It was a low-key, swanky spot with pretty good food and even better drinks. I figured if he turned out to be a dud, I could get drunk and still have a pretty decent time.

I had a general amount of nervousness as I parked the car. I had texted him and told him I was pulling up. I ended up running a little late for our first date. He replied "OK," so I couldn't tell if he was irritated or not. I walked into the restaurant and didn't see him. Well, I didn't see any black guys at first, so I'm thinking to myself that he might've stood me up. He was actually already seated upstairs on the second level. I was hoping he had at least ordered himself a drink since I was about twenty minutes late. As the hostess escorted me to the table, I was secretly hoping he wasn't fat. I never asked him what he looked like over the phone because I didn't want to seem shallow. He was in the music industry, plus he had shared with me that his cousin was an NBA player, so I knew he had more than enough experience dealing with superficial girls. I approached the booth, and I was caught off guard by the physical appearance of the man seated in front of me. When I say he was picture perfect, wow. He stood up to greet me and seeing him in full view made my pussy jump. He was at least 6'4", chocolate, I mean the perfect most even dark skin tone I had ever seen. His body was perfect; not skinny but not a muscle man either. He had nice broad shoulders I could see through his tee shirt, and to top it off, he was wearing army fatigue pants. I had this secret obsession with anything army fatigue. I said a silent thank you prayer to the "game gods." (The "game gods" was a term I had made up years ago for anytime things went right or I needed extra help in the man department. I prayed to them. They were my secret weapon and seemed to always look out for me.)

After a short hug we both sat down, he complimented my outfit; for the evening I was wearing this white distressed tank top from Urban Outfitters. It was a crew neck, but some of the holes showed a little bit of my bare skin. Since my little weight loss, my C cups sat up perfect, so I was leaving a bra at home most of the time. I had on these skinny jeans and some strappy nude-colored sandals. He let me know that he appreciated the fact that I had beautiful feet. He also liked that I was wearing nude nail polish on my toes that complimented my shoes and skin tone. His voice alone was enough to make any woman melt, but the way he spoke was its own type of seductive. Every single thing he said glided out of his mouth with so much confidence. He had perfect speech and even more perfect teeth. I ordered a cosmo, and we ordered our food as well. I took notice that he didn't order a drink for himself and later found out he didn't drink. He was actually a little bothered by the fact that I drank. He said he let me live since it was our first date. I never drank in front of him again after that day. Needless to say our first date went every well, minus the liquor. Industry and I had a lot in common. We both loved music and fashion. We both had a really deep side to us, and we shared a common need for separation in our personal lives. I was at a point in my life where I felt very misunderstood by most of my family and friends, and he was at a similar place in his own life. It didn't take long before the two of us were spending every available moment on the phone texting and sharing our day-to-day lives with one another. He was back and forth between NYC and Philly a lot, so when he told me he was coming to town, I dropped everything to spend time with him.

When he came to town, he stayed at his mother's house in south Philly. He was an only child, so I think his mom just let him do whatever he wanted. Even at 28 years old, I could tell she loved him so much that she was just happy to have him around when he was there. I normally wouldn't ever deal with a guy living at his mom's house, but he wasn't really living there. Plus, I knew how much he traveled, so for I made a n exception. He had transformed a room in the house into a recording studio. He produced music, so he told me he needed a space to be creative in at all times. Just in case something came to mind, he could get in there and record it. He also had a little apartment-style area setup in the basement of the house. It was like a little secret hideout he created for himself. Once you waked down those steps, it was like you were in another world. The bed room area was very dark and there was nothing in the room but a large bed and a TV. The TV was brand new, but it had dust on it. I could tell he never used it.

Our evenings together were started to get intense. I wasn't able to just go eat and head our separate ways. My sexual desire for him grew by the second, so I knew this time around I was going to end up giving him some action. I had been in the bedroom before, so I walked down stairs and sat on the bed. He came into the room with a glass of ice and his own bottle of water. He knew me pretty well by now and knew that I enjoyed eating ice cubes. He took his shirt off, exposing his toned chest and large arms. I was not giving this body enough credit. He looked so good topless. He laid in bed with his head propped on the pillows and signaled for me to start undressing as well. I took off my shirt without hesitation. This day, I was wearing a bra. I left it on, but I took my pants off. I never wore underwear, so my entire pink waxed pussy was now exposed as well.

Since I was now so accustomed to being the first one to make a move, I started to stroke his penis through his boxer briefs. He allowed me to stroke him for a few minutes, but then he instructed me to come and kiss his chest. I didn't reject him. I placed my full wet lips on his lower abs and kissed him slowly from his belly button up to his neck. He pushed my mouth in the direction of his nipples. I wasn't sure if he wanted them licked or sucked so I started to lick them gently. He told me to bite them; he wanted to feel some pain. So that's what I did. I bit down on his nipples, gripping the skin with my front teeth. I allowed a lot of spit to drip out of my mouth and continued to lick his erect nipples until his penis was about to jump through his boxers. Performing oral sex was one of my biggest talents. Looking at his huge dick stand up in those boxers was making my mouth water even more. I couldn't resist the urge to grab hold of it and wrap my lips around it. As I approached the lower part of his body, he lifted himself up so I could slide the boxers off him. His area was shaved, and his dick looked like a big black candy bar I couldn't wait to taste.

I was now facing him looking dead into his eyes. Making eye contact with my victims had become another one of my favorite parts of oral sex as well. I gathered a ton on spit in my mouth and allowed it all to spill onto his dick. I watched his eyes as they followed the spit exiting my lips and falling onto his manhood. I saw how much he enjoyed it, so that was my signal to go ahead and start eating my candy. I licked both sides of it, creating a slippery mess as I switched back and forth from the left side back to the right side. The final time I stopped and licked his dick straight up the middle and landing the entire mushroom cap head in my mouth. His dick glided down my throat like a straw. I allowed him to watch me insert the whole nine plus inches and then released it back to him. I placed his hands on it. I wanted to see him stroke himself. I loved to see a man touch himself.

By now my pussy was dripping onto his leg. I was still facing him as we both tag teamed his dick. He grabbed me up by my armpits and positioned me on top of him. The candy bar went into my hole with ease, but he filled my insides up completely. At first my knees were resting at the sides, but once I felt the pressure of him inside me, I needed it to go deeper, so I stood up on my feet and begun to ride him at a fast pace. His eyes were closed the entire time. I knew he could feel my pussy creaming onto his dick as I jumped up and down on him like a wild animal. When he was about to explode he threw me off him, and my body dropped to the opposite side of the bed. I pointed to my mouth and ran my index finger across my lips and opened my mouth. He exploded right between my lips, every drop of him dancing on my tongue. He tasted even better than he felt. I proceeded to swallow his juices, grabbed a blanket, rolled over, and slept like a baby. I learned a few things that night about Industry. He was a bit of a freak asking me to bite those nipples. Even agreeing to shoot in my mouth, I wasn't impressed with him too much, but I was hoping the next time around he would show me a little bit more of what he had inside. I could tell there was more to him sexually, and I wasn't sure why he was holding back.

Industry didn't drink. He didn't party. He didn't really do anything besides work and travel. I always wanted to ask him what made him so reserved and boring, but he had this way of intimidating me, so I really wasn't big on speaking up. I had no idea why I was so nervous around him. I mean, I allowed him to get to know me for who I was. Plus, I think he done a little hood homework on me, so the few times I attempted to downplay some of my character, he pretty much let me know he already knew all about me. I guess it did feel good not to have to be fake for once. He was really a good guy, and I wanted to show him that even though people viewed me as wild and maybe even a little easy, I could be faithful and wasn't just this sex-crazed, money-hungry chick people made me out to be. The two of us became really close, really fast. It had only been a few months, and I had cut all my other dudes off. I even changed my cell phone number. I was starting to think that he might be "the one." I was going crazy. My family and friends even noticed I was acting different. Industry had everything going for him.

He also had some secret addictions that made our interaction get really intense. He had a crazy foot fetish; he loved my feet.

He liked for me to only wear nude nail polish on my toes, and he requested that they be done on a weekly basis. He would randomly text me throughout the day and ask me to send him photos of my feet. Even during sex he would request for my feet to be on his chest or he would want me to rub my feet across his body as he stroked his dick. My feet quickly became the star of our foreplay. I was once again becoming the object of a man's sexual desires, and of course it made me feel powerful. I was learning that every man could be controlled; all you had to do is find out what his kink was. You just had to use that as your way to get him to do whatever you wanted. For a while I was able to deal with Industry on my terms. He was my main guy, but I still called the shots. I made myself available to him only when I wanted to. I was still able to play a little cat and mouse with him. Sometimes he called and I would pretend I was out of town. I wouldn't answer his text messages. I acted like I didn't get them. I maintained a level of independence in my personal life. I felt like it was important not to ever allow a man to feel like you needed him. Even if that meant I wasn't going to see him for a few days, even if not seeing him was the last thing I wanted to do, I stood my ground. I played my game.

We had a very active sex life. I was able to get him to break out of his shell more and more each time. His requests started to become more erotic, and I was loving every minute of it. Being involved with a man that wasn't scared to explore his sexuality was like a dream come true for me. During oral he would let me venture off to his asshole. I would start sucking his dick, catering to his perfect shaped head and rim. Industry had to have one of the most attractive penis I ever saw, and sucking it became one of my favorite things to do. As my lips made their way along the sides, I'd leave a slippery path of salvia, creating a pool of liquid down his entire shaft. He loved for me to keep it really wet and nasty, so I would get down to his balls and juggle them in mouth, allowing them to bounce off my tongue. The liquid would be flowing uncontrollably out of my mouth by the time I got to his ass. My tongue would escape into his asshole, and I would slightly blow into it. His knees would jerk from the sensation I created, and he moaned for me. His moan was my drug. I needed to know he was enjoying my work. Pleasing his asshole sent chills through my entire body. My pussy would leak as soon he reached the peak of his pleasure. It didn't take long for him to request me on top of him, and he would begin to punish me for the big mess I made all over his body.

One night, the pace of our sexual encounter was a little different. Instead of starting it off by rubbing my feet on his chest and giving his nipples the attention they required, he asked me to take all my clothes off and lay on the bed. I was a little hesitant at first, but I did it. He pulled out a black bandana and started to tie my hands together. I was loving his sudden need to take the lead. He placed his finger over his lip and told me not to say a word. I listened as he started to suck on my breast. I was never really into men sucking my titties, but it felt good. I wasn't sure if it was just because it was him or the fact that I was tied up. Either way I was loving every second of it. He feasted on my breasts for a little while and then he got up and looked me in my eyes. He said to me, "I noticed how wet your pussy gets while my dick is inside you, but you always make me stop before you're able to fully climax. I know you have it in you to squirt, so tonight I'm going to make you squirt. And I'm not stopping until you do."

"Squirt?" I asked.

"Yes, squirt. I saw your pussy jumping. I know you can do it."

Secretly, he was right. I could squirt, but I had no idea it was something men enjoyed. I had grown to be very ashamed of the pools of liquid that would shoot out of my body, so i stopped allowing myself to do it. I would always stop before it leaked out. My trips to the restroom after sex would became very important for me. I had done a really good job hiding my ability up until now. I could tell in his eyes he wasn't joking. He was about to take things to a whole other level, and I couldn't even stop him. He placed his finger inside me, and massaging my insides slowly, he used his pointer finger to flick my clit. It didn't take long before my juices started to flow onto his hands. He placed two more fingers inside me. Once he noticed that he had reached my spot, he applied more pressure, forcing his long fingers inside my hole and causing my pussy to tighten up. He started attacking my clit, plucking it faster and faster. By this time my legs were shaking, and I was letting out the most intense sounds of pleasure. Then he put his face in it. He kept his finger inside as he sucked on my clit. I could feel this warm numbness on the inside and I knew he was about to take me into a place I had been rejecting for so long. The blood was rushing to my head as he pounded my insides with so much force. His tongue was racing along my clit. My head was spinning. I had lost all control of my body. I couldn't do anything to stop the rush if I wanted to. All of a sudden I felt a river of liquid drain from inside me. I was overcome with satisfaction, and his entire face was dripping with my juice. He laughed as he got up, looked me in my eyes, licked his lips, and went back down for more. This time he sucked on my clit and forced half his hand inside me. The combination of pain and pleasure was overwhelming. My body continued to convulse.

I showered him at least half dozen times that night, the whole experience felt like a dream. I didn't believe my body could do it. I had laid on my back for hours shooting liquid from my pussy without warning. I knew I could squirt, but I never knew it could be like this. Our encounters had become so much more intense after that night. He would let me get in the bed without layering it with bath towels to absorb the buckets of juice I had become a pro at ejecting. Within months he had me to the point that he didn't even have to touch me anymore. I would stand straight up, play with my nipples, and squirt. Just stand there and the juice would escape. He turned on a button inside my pussy that I had been able to control for so long. He had also taught me a whole new level of power. Now that I could squirt on demand, I had another advantage over most chicks my age. None of my girlfriends could squirt. This was a rare a skill, and I was so happy to have Industry around to teach me everything I needed to know about my new weapon.

I was completely turned out by the time winter came around. Our sexual relationship had become so intense. I hate to admit that he had a hold over me. Within a year I had changed my phone number, I even bought a sidekick phone so we could text each other faster. I gave him a special ringtone; when I heard it I would rush to my phone. I never told him no, ever. Anything he asked me to do, I did it. I was at his mercy. The feeling I felt when I was around him was magical. He could just look at me, and I would drip in my pants. Both his love for music and his ability to work my body over made me fall for him bad. I had become so blinded by the sex I wasn't paying attention to the fact that more than a year had past, and we had never had a serious conversation about the status of our situation. This was one of the only times I was with a man that didn't take care of me financially. Yes, he would pay when we went out and even do little things out of kindness, but he never put cash in my hands. We had even took our situation bi-coastal and spent time with each other in L.A. He had moved over there to do his music, and I was doing my own thing on the west coast as well. The time we spent in L.A. was pretty much just like our time in Philly. We would meet up, eat, chat, and fuck. Our sexual chemistry was so intense, I started to fall in love with him. I had completely lost control and allowed him to be everything to me. His voice alone would change my mood, but it didn't take long before the sex was no longer enough. We weren't connecting on a deeper level. I was wasting my time. I never really expressed to him how I felt. I kind of allowed his busy schedule and my fake busy career to get in the way.

We parted ways on a good note. There was no bad blood. But I felt so stupid in the end. I mean I had given so much of my power to him. Industry had me wrapped around his finger, or really wrapped around his penis. I couldn't believe I stayed with him so long, and I was actually faithful to him and he wasn't even my man.

I know now it wasn't even him I was devoting myself to; it was the sex. Before him I had never equated sex with emotions. I was obviously not a virgin, but I had never really been in love. I programed my brain at a young age. I refused to end up one of those lonely girls crying over a guy. Since I was about 13 I was attracting older men. They all said the same thing, "You're so pretty… let me take care of you," knowing damn well they only wanted sex. That's what pissed me off the most about men. They all only wanted sex. Even if you met a guy that showed you affection or took you out on fancy dates, nine times out of ten he was only doing it to get you to sleep with him. I hated men for that very reason. So the whole situation I got in with Industry had me feeling like a fool. I knew better then to get all caught up, but it was too late. I spent weeks crying over him. My friends even noticed how sad I was, I couldn't eat. I was barley sleeping. I would sit in my room and replay the last year and a half in my head, which made it even worse. I had the reputation of being very cold and usually unaffected by men. They came and went. As long as I got what I wanted (usually money and gifts) then I was fine. I never worried about who else they were dealing with. He could have a wife and two other mistresses for all I cared. Men only wanted one thing, and so did I. it was an even exchange up until now.

So after like a month of feeling stupid I got myself back together. I was ready to get back in the game. I had a new mindset and nobody was about to take me off track ever again.

January 2008

There was something about watching him pound on another bitch, bending her over and gliding his penis inside her... watching him in action became one of my favorite things to do. Last night was no different, well maybe a little different...

Bee is my best friend. Well. my best guy friend. We became really close over the past five years. It started out as just a simple friendship. He would see me out and pay my tabs. We would talk here and there, and we found out we had much in common. He was like the male version of me. It didn't take long for us to get close. I loved that I was able to count on him for advice and money. I never really looked at Bee in a sexual way. He was always just like a brother to me. Not that he wasn't handsome, because he was. Standing a little over six feet tall with a muscular build, his caramel complexion was always shining because he loved to lather cocoa butter on his face and body. He kept his hair cut really low and had the demeanor of a boss. Like a Jay-Z type of guy. College educated but street swag that made him capture the attention of every female in the room. Bee and I had started having threesomes a few years ago, ironically in Atlantic City.

He had a gambling problem, so he was basically living off his comps at the Borgata Casino. He invited me to come hang out one night, and I brought my girlfriend Aaliyah along for the ride. We had dinner and way too many shots of Patron and ended up in his suite. Aaliyah was way more drunk than me. She went right in and took her clothes off. Bee approached her and she unbuttoned his pants and started sucking his dick. She went wild on his dick, soaking it with saliva. She moaned from the enjoyment, and I too started to get really moist. I had to join in… I walked over towards them, and she threw me on the bed. She yanked my leggings down and started eating my pussy. Her warm lips felt so good that I started to moan as well. Bee had this look in his eyes that I had never seen before. He was under a spell. I gestured for him to fuck her, and that's just what he did. She was on all fours eating me out and Bee pulled me by my arms up to the top of the king size bed. My head rested on the pillow as she lay between my legs and continued to make my pussy drip . Bee got behind her and started pounding on her pussy. I don't know if it was the sound of her screams or the fact that the harder he pounded her the more aggressively she chewed on my pussy. Whatever it was, I couldn't control myself, and I exploded into her mouth. My pussy released like a gushing water fountain. She didn't even stop as I squirted down her throat; she swallowed all of me. Bee continued to fuck her, and eventually he fucked me too. It was a crazy night that changed our relationship forever.

After that night Bee and I started having sex a lot. We had a crazy connection. He would enter me, and my body would just explode. He would touch me, and my body would get wet. We were able to enjoy sex and still have a good friendship. It was the definition of "no strings attached." After a few months, he started to introduce me to his "girlfriends." They all loved me, and eventually we started having sex with them together. Our sessions were amazing. I was able to satisfy my craving for control, get some good dick, and get my pussy ate all while watching him pleasure another woman.

I had a funny feeling pulling up to the Aloft. I mean, this was clearly not the first time Bee had me meet him and one of his female friends at a hotel, but this time I wasn't really in the mood. He was asking me to do something that I was 100% uncomfortable with, with someone I had never looked at in a sexual way. I hated her. I hated what she represented. She was his son's mother, April. I know I shouldn't even be doing this shit. He had a hold on me though. I just couldn't tell him no. Sitting in the parking lot, I tried to convince myself I wasn't crazy. I practiced my facial expressions and my body language. See, April didn't know that Bee and I had been sexual partners for the past few years. She didn't know about the time we spent alone together, how he would tell me how much he loves me and wants me to have his baby. She was clueless to the fact that he had flown me places, so we could go on dates without being seen. She just thought that we were close friends. Supposedly she had requested this threesome. She's had this major girl crush on me and she "heard" I had a really wet pussy. They were out drinking and he texted me, told me about her wish , and like a fool, I agreed to meet them.

When I walked in, he was in the shower. *Shit, now I have to talk to her.* I had all kinds of shit running through my mind. April sat on the bed with this childish smirk on her face. Her legs looked so skinny in her jeans. One of the things I disliked most about April was her size. She was so little, so very thin that her body looked like a preteen. I don't know how she could take all that dick Bee was packing. I mean, I know that shit has to hurt. It hurt me. I broke the silence as I walked over and gave her a hug. She pointed over to the table with an extra-large bottle of Grey Goose and a couple cans of coke. I was so happy to see the liquor. I was gonna have to get really drunk to go through with this shit. I poured myself a huge shot, then another, and then I made me a cocktail with the coke. By then Bee was coming out of the bathroom wearing only a towel.

"Yo, cuz," he spoke. I just nodded my head. He walked over towards me and grabbed the bottle of Goose and took a huge gulp straight outta the bottle. April came and hugged him from behind. *Uggggh.* Shit was getting more and more awkward by the minute. The three of us had a couple more shots, laughed about some local gossip, and made small talk. About an hour had past, and I was ready to get things started. This was the part that I was worried about the most. I couldn't walk over to Bee and start sucking his dick because then she would realize we had done this before. I had to play third wheel and wait for them to start fucking before I could jump in. Bee laid on the bed and took his towel off. April walked towards him, and the closer she got to him, the more clothes she removed. First her shirt, then her jeans. She had the smallest ass I had ever seen on an adult. Her spine visible in her boney back. She just didn't look like a grown woman. She started to take her bra off, and to my surprise, she actually had beautiful breast. I can't front. Her boobs were perfect, small, full, and very perky.

Bee started sucking on her perfect breast as she stood over him. He quickly tossed her body onto the bed and started finger fucking her while never taking his mouth off her breast. She began to moan. Normally at this point I would be taking charge, but I had to remain in my seat, watching from the sideline. April laid across the bed and tooted her tiny ass in the air. She was ready for that pounding. Bee looked back at me and gestured for me to join. I was wearing a powder blue Juicy sweat suit with only my bra underneath, no panties on. As I walked towards the bed, I unzipped my hoodie and exposed my hot pink bra. By the time I reached the bed, April was holding her arm out. She grasped my thigh and let me know that she wanted me to lay in front of her with my pussy facing her mouth. I got in position, still wearing my pants, and I laid there staring at the celling for about 90 seconds. That's when I felt her pulling my pants down.

She started to pat my pussy, rubbing it and admiring the clean wax I had. My clit was poking out as usual, so she began to rub her fingers on it, making me moist right away. Bee noticed that she was playing with my pussy, so he inserted himself into her from behind. She let out the loudest scream I had ever heard. His thick dick had made contact with her, and I could only imagine how much pain she was in. Her tiny ass couldn't possibly take all of him. April spread my pussy open and gave it a wet kiss. My clit was pulsating; her mouth felt good. It was cool and wet. The harder Bee pounded her, the more aggressively she ate me. I was ready to come, but for some reason I was nervous. Did she know I was a squirter?

She had no idea what was about to take place. I knew I had to hold back, at least for now. Bee turned her over and kissed all my juices off her face. I wanted him so bad. I wanted him to bend me over next, but he didn't. He laid back as she started to suck his dick. I didn't move until she gave me permission to join her. I started sucking his balls while April concentrated on his dick. She was being so selfish. The moment she stopped for air, I wrapped my lips around his dick. I allowed the spit to drip down his shaft. I started to tease his head with my tongue. Bee loved that shit. His eyes began to roll into the back of his head. I knew he was in heaven. I had long since mastered the art of sucking his dick. It was finally my time to shine, and as Bee was about to cum, he jumped up to get me to stop. He bent April over once again and started fucking her. I was pissed. I wanted to feel him inside me so bad, my pussy was jumping, my clit was throbbing, but nothing. No dick for me.

April made eye contact with me and whispered how she wanted to taste me again, so I got in position and allowed her one more taste. She was eating my kitten like candy, taking her time with my clit this time around. She moved her tongue inside me with such precision. As much as I hated her, she was making my body feel so I couldn't hold back anymore. I had to let go. *Oh god.* I was holding my stomach in, trying really hard not to explode, but it was too late. Bee let out a mild grunt, and I knew he was about to climax. I took a deep breath, closed my eyes, and let go. A river rushed out of my body. April looked up at me with my liquid running down her face, dripping from her hair. I had ruined her bangs; they were stuck to her face. She winked at me and went back down for more. She flicked my clit with her index finger. She literally begged for more, saying "Come on, baby. Rain for me." She kept repeating it, "Rain for me. Make this pussy rain!" So that's just what I did April drank three rounds of my juice. She had turned into another person right before my eyes. I always looked at her as this shy, square chick. I would have never guessed she could be so sexual. Bee had never mentioned her in this way. It was my squirt that did that to people. Either you hated it or you fell in love with it. April was in love with it.

Our session ended and Bee and April laid in the bed naked. She laid satisfied right in the puddle I had created, and I went to the bathroom to wash off and put my clothes back on. April wanted me to stay, but I had had enough. Feeling very strange, I had mixed emotions. I was definitely satisfied sexually, but my head was pounding. I declined the offer, grabbed my keys and purse, and left. The entire ride home, I cried. Tears flowed down my face, and I didn't even understand why. I had a heart full of jealously, anger, and pain. I couldn't believe Bee didn't fuck me. I had been in a secret relationship with this man for years, and I had never felt rejection from him or any man really. I felt sick. I needed to get my mind right. I allowed Bee to use me for his own sexual pleasures dozens of times, so why was this time so different? Watching him fuck April made me so upset. Hearing her say she loved him during sex and hearing him repeat it back was too much. Their words echoed in my mind, my head continued pounding more and more each minute. I had to get my mind off Bee and that bitch…

***

I ignored Bees calls for about a week after our episode with April. He kept texting me, letting me know that she was asking for me. She wanted to link up again. But I just couldn't put myself back in that position. That definitely had to end as a one-night stand. Seeing Bee with her kilt me. I couldn't stomach him kissing her and the look in her eyes as he fucked her. I knew April was really in love with him, and despite all the things he had been telling me about her, he was in love with her too. All these years I had convinced myself that it was okay for Bee and I to have our little secret relationship. Truth is, I was playing myself. I let him have 100% of my mind and body. Whenever he called I would answer. Whatever he wanted me to do, I did. I was allowing him to have his cake and eat it too. I didn't feel comfortable being the loser in this situation. I had to come up with a plan to get the upper hand again. Bee wasn't just some random guy. He really was one of my closest friends, and I didn't want to lose the friendship. Yet, I also didn't want to fuck April ever again. How was I going to tell him, "Game over?"

A few days had gone by, and I hadn't heard anything from Bee. I wasn't ready to have the "no more threesomes" conversation, so not hearing from him was actually a good thing. I looked for ways to keep him off my mind. So when my girlfriend Dana asked me to go out, I was all for it. The club scene had changed so much and people were starting to hang in little lounges and even in the strip clubs. Dana said we were going to Dalilah's, one of the most high-end strip clubs in the entire city. The food there was five star and females couldn't even come inside unless accompanied by a man. I questioned her about how we were going to get in, and she told me she would call her "Big Bro." He knew the staff there very well, and we would definitely be let in. We arrived to the overcrowded parking lot about at about ten. Dana wasn't really a good dresser. She never looked a total mess, but her clothes were rather cheap. She'd wear a whole outfit from the Rainbow shop like it was designer. On the other hand, I was raised by well-dressed women. I always made sure I looked good, even on a casual day. I would consider this very casual; I wasn't the type of girl to try to upstage the strippers. I was very careful about dressing overly sexy in the strip clubs. Dana had on a low-budget tee shirt with something written on the front and some jeans. I wore this red jumpsuit I had sitting in my closet for a while now, long sleeve with a keyhole in the back, body hugging but not too tight. I dressed it down with some all-white Chuck Taylors. We looked like we were going to two different venues, but she was my friend, and I respected her for never trying to be something she wasn't.

Big Bro pulled up about ten minutes after us in an all-black Ford pickup. You could hear his mouth before he parked his car. "Dana!" he yelled.

I stepped out of the car and started walking towards the front of the club. Dana got out too; she didn't even acknowledge the fact that he was screaming at her from his car window.

"Dana!" he screamed again. This time she turned around and signaled with her hand for him to walk over towards us.

Big Bro was older, likely in his early 40s. Tall and medium built, he wasn't really cute, but he wasn't ugly either. He was well dressed, though, with a designer shirt, nice jeans, and sneakers. He had the classic North Philly low cut and a beard, but not one of the big beards. His was well groomed. That's how I could tell he was a little older. He looked me up and down. He didn't bother to introduce himself, just looked at me and nodded his head for us to follow him in. We walked in, and Big Bro was like a celebrity. Everybody smiled and greeted him like he owned the place, and we ended up sitting up in the VIP section. I had been here a dozen times, but I never sat upstairs. It was cool to be treated so well. He said we could order whatever we wanted. Dana went crazy getting damn near everything on the menu, and we were ordering so many drinks I lost count. I even got a shoulder and back massage; it felt so good. He stayed there until it closed. Big Bro had at least six different guys come meet him there. They would sit and talk to him and leave. I recognized one or two of them, but once the Grey Goose started to kick in, the faces became a blur. Well dressed or not, Dana was good for a night out!

We all walked to the parking lot. Well I tip toed to the car, still feeling my drinks but trying not to look drunk. I didn't want to embarrass myself in front of all those people. I sat in the passenger seat, and as I tried to close the door, Big Bro was standing there with his phone in his hand talking about "put my number in his phone." I laughed a little bit and gave him my number. The whole ride home Dana kept saying how she knew he liked me. She coached me on how to get him to fuck with me, but the whole time I'm just thinking she must be crazy. I didn't need nobody to tell me how to get a nigga to like me. Obviously what I was doing was working. He said about two words to me all night and wouldn't let me leave without getting my number. Big Bro was already fucking with me; she just didn't dig it.

Three days later...

I pulled up to the Chart House on Delaware Ave to have dinner with Big Bro. I lived in Philly all my life and had never ate here. I didn't really know what to expect because I still never really had a full conversation with him. He had called me the day after our strip club meet-up and asked if I was free tonight. He was already inside, and he called me twice since I pulled up, yelling in the phone and asking, "Where you at?" I walked into the Chart House in a black dress and some animal printed pumps. I was trying to keep it simple, but I wanted to look a little classy since we were eating on the water front. Big Bro was sitting at a corner table. He still wore his hat on his head and was already eating. I was irked but quickly remembered he was from North Philly, so the last thing I should have expected was for him to be a gentleman. "Bout time," he said as I sat down, damn near yelling at me.

I giggled and said some shit like, "Good things come to those who wait," or something corny like that. He smiled. I knew he was just talking shit. Plus, I wasn't that late. He ordered me a drink, and I ordered my food as we started to converse about different things. At first, I thought he was all hood, but once I started talking to him, I learned he was kind of a good guy. He had a few kids and was making moves in the city. I never asked how he got his money because that's never any of my business. But I made it very clear to him that I didn't really date street guys and wasn't about to be riding shotgun with no drug dealers. He thought I was crazy and that was the night he gave me my nickname "Hollywood."

We finished dinner and he asked me if I wanted to hang out. I didn't mind. Dinner was cool and we were actually getting along. He didn't say much, but it was important when he did. From our hour conversation over dinner, I felt like he had a clear understanding of what type of chick I was. We arrived at this club called Fusion off of Spring Garden Street in downtown Philly. It was almost like he owned the place. He rode in my car to the club, and we pulled up to valet with no wait and walked straight into the doors. He walked up top to the VIP area and spoke to every single person in the building, including the owner, who he felt the need to introduce me to. We had a ball in the club, and by the time two in the morning rolled around, I was done. Like I damn near couldn't even walk. Somehow, I managed to drive us a few blocks over to Market Street to the Omni, which I later learned was like Big Bro's second home. I stumbled out the driver seat and walked onto the elevator. He wasn't too sober himself. I could tell by the way he was looking at me that he was drunk. His eyes were red, and he had sweat on the tip of his nose. The hotel suite was beautiful, almost regal looking. I went straight to the bathroom, forced my finger down my throat, and made myself throw up. I rinsed my mouth out and went back into the bedroom. He was already in his boxers in bed. I took my shoes off and walked toward the opposite side of the bed to lay down. I didn't take my dress off. I wasn't wearing any underwear and wasn't about to be all loose on the first night. We both passed out. The next morning, he woke me up asking me to drop him off. I didn't mind. I was just happy I made it through night one without giving him some. I took him to this little block in North Philly, and before he got out the car he handed me a couple hundred and told me he would see me later.

Later that evening we linked back up at the strip club. He called it "the office." He was already inside, but this time when I got to the door, the security walked me right in and showed me his table. I sat beside him, and he didn't even look me in my face. He was too busy talking to the bartender. He ordered me a drink, and I sat there quietly for about thirty minutes before he finally grabbed my hand and asked me. "What up." Big Bro had this way about him where he didn't have to say too much. He was a boss, and I could tell from day one that he wasn't used to women that challenged him. He liked that I had something to say, that he couldn't just tell me what to do, even though after only a couple days I could see how another female would be so caught up that she would be doing just about anything for this man. He knew I wasn't that type of girl. He had to treat me right. I wasn't that easy, I think he liked that about me.

Two weeks later...

Dana told me the whole city was talking about me and Big Bro. She also told me his girl was some crazy bitch from the other side of town and she heard he was fucking with me too. I wasn't worried. It had been a few weeks and me and Big Bro had been everywhere together. This girlfriend couldn't be too important if he had me on his arm from state to state as we spent damn near every night together. I told Dana I didn't give a fuck, and if a bitch wanted a problem they could get it. I was more concerned with the notion of the whole city knowing who I was dealing with. Don't get me wrong, he was a cool dude, but I had always been the private type. I wasn't really into people knowing my business.

When I met up with him that night I mentioned the stuff Dana said about the girlfriend and all that. He laughed at me and told me to chill, he had it under control, and I didn't have anything to worry about. We ended our night at the Omni and up until now he never seemed to want anything from me sexually. But this night the vibe was way different. We kissed a few times on the elevator, and by the time we were in the suite his dick was visibly hard through his jeans. I don't know what was in the Grey Goose that night, but I was witnessing that side of him for the first time.

He fumbled onto the bed, and taking his shirt off, he gestured for me to take off his boots, so I did. His pants came off next. By the time his pants fell to the floor, I was standing on top of him wearing only my bra. He pulled my body close to him and started kissing on my neck. I could feel his dick pressed up against my pussy through his boxers. It was big. I was ready, but he flipped me on my back before I could start taking control. He kissed my body really slow from my neck to my tits and down to my pussy. It was dripping wet before his mouth touched it. He sucked on my clit a little bit and proceeded to take his boxers off. I wasn't about to let him take full control, so sild down to the bottom of the bed and came back up between his legs and started sucking the head of his hard dick, making the saliva in my mouth create rings of water on the head. He was moaning. I loved that sound. He tried to lift up, but I placed my hand on his chest and told him to relax. I continued to feast on his long thick dick until I felt that vein start to throb. I knew he was about ready to explode, so I stopped and grabbed his left hand and pulled it towards my pussy. I wanted him to feel how wet it was, the liquid dripping down his index finger. I noticed the gold condom package on the side of bed, so I grabbed it, and he placed it on his dick. He entered me, and it felt like a truck had drove inside my body. His thick dick created this intense pressure, and I couldn't control myself. My legs started to shake after a few strong strokes, and I felt a rush a fluid come showering down from inside me. I couldn't stop it. As my pussy exploded all over the both us the bed was soaked and so were we. He jumped up so fast, ripped the condom off his dick, and threw it at me. He looked at me in my eyes and yelled, "What the FUCK!?" so loud I was sure the whole hotel could hear him. I was so embarrassed. I mean, here I was in the middle of a major climax and he hated it! Big Bro went into the bathroom and came out with all the towels he could find, wrapped himself in one, and sat on the edge of the bed. He turned his back to me and didn't say another word. I eventually got up, washed off, and put my clothes back on. I slept on the sofa that night, and he slept on the corner of the water bed I had created.

The next morning was the most awkward moment of my life. No one said a word for like an hour. Finally, he said, "Hollywood, I done had sex with a ton of bitches, but never in my life have I ever saw nothing like that. I'm not with that freak shit."

"That freak shit?" I asked. He went on and on about how no pussy wasn't about to drive him crazy and how he don't like that squirting shit. He wasn't feeling it and made it clear that we wouldn't be fucking again for a while.

I felt bad after that encounter with Big Bro. I had never had anyone deny me dick. But we kept fucking around even though we weren't that sexually active. I would suck his dick a lot, but I can't lie, I was starting to crave some dick. A few months went by and Big Bro was really taking good care of me. He bought me whatever I wanted, we were eating at all the five-star places in the city, and he even threw me a little party for my birthday. I didn't have a thing to complain about except the sex.

A few days after my birthday, Big Bro and I were at the office having drinks when I thought I saw a ghost. I looked up to see him shaking hands with Bee. I couldn't believe it. I had been ignoring his calls and avoiding him for months. I don't know why, but I tried to hide my face, thinking they would shake hands and Bee would go on about his business. Before the thought could process, Big Bro was introducing me to my own best friend. I got up out of my seat and gave Bee a hug. I told Big Bro we already knew each other, that Bee was like my brother. He looked at me like I was crazy but didn't say a word. Bee tapped me on my ass and told me I needed to call his phone.

The next day I'm pacing the floor in Nia's apartment, trying to tell her the quick version of the last few months of my life. She knew all about Bee and our crazy relationship, but I had never told her about the situation with April (the baby momma) mostly because I was so embarrassed. I was still very mad at myself for putting myself in that type of predicament. But Nia was never judgmental. That's one of the reasons we clicked. At this point I didn't know what to do. Bee had his girls, and I'm sure he figured that I had my niggaz, but he had never saw me out with anyone. Plus, all I could picture is the look in his eyes when he realized it was me sitting at the bar with Big Bro. I felt like I owed him some type of explanation Shit, I had been ignoring his calls for weeks. Nia felt differently about the whole situation. She was always on some "fuck niggaz, get money" shit. And I really can't blame her. It seems like the minute you start trusting and even liking one of these guys here comes the bullshit. So after my dramatic story telling and a few glasses of wine, we decided that it was best that I call Bee before too much time passed.

So I texted him right away.

"Yo."

Bee: "Where you at?"

"Down north."

Bee: "Nia crib?"

"Yup."

Bee: "You dress?"

"Yeah."

Bee: "Well I'm coming to grab you, I need you to take a ride with me."

Bee pulls up in record time. I kiss Nia goodbye and walk outside. I can't even fully get in the seat before he starts snapping. "What the fuck you doing fucking with Big Bro? He's a nut ass old-head. You know better than that."

Bee was going on and on about how Big Bro is a nut, he ain't getting no money, I better not be fucking him, and you know he fuck with that crazy bitch… blah blah blah. I was just sitting there being scolded like a child. Finally, he gave me the opportunity to speak, and I explained to him that I met him through my girlfriend Dana and he was an alright dude to me. I told him we really just been kicking it, eating, drinking, hanging out. I even told him about the squirt disaster. I was telling him way too much. He thought it was funny and told me I was crazy. Bee never had anything to say about me and no other nigga, so I looked at it like it could only be two different things. Either he really didn't think Big Bro was a good look or he as jealous. It could have been a little bit of both. Either way, seeing him this upset was turning me on. I never saw this side of him. All the time this back and forth conversation was going on I didn't even notice we were in Delaware. We pulled up to this single-family home, Bee opened the garage from the inside of the car, and we pulled in. I was still not saying a word. Bee gestured for me to get out, so I walked straight into the kitchen space with its beautiful white marble counter tops and classic black and white floors so clean I could see my reflection. Making my way through to the living room, it was just as nice. The house was furnished with grand modern style furniture paintings on the wall. It reminded me of scene in a music video. This house was just sexy. I asked Bee whose house we were in. He said it's his, and

I'm thinking he's lying, but he never lied to me. So for the moment, I chose to believe him.

Fifteen minutes later, we ended up in the master bed room. Bee loved to lay up. I started taking my clothes off so we could get in the bed. I noticed a huge tub in the master bathroom, so I asked he wanted to take a bath. I ran the water extra hot, added some bubbles, and Bee and I laid together in the bath. It almost felt romantic. He played with my hair as I lay between his legs on his chest. He washed my back and kissed my feet. I washed his whole body head to toe. I stopped at this penis and sucked the bubbles off. We both dried off and got into the bed naked.

Riding back home, all I could think about was Big Bro. I couldn't believe I let Bee fuck me again. I was trying to get over him, but when we got around each other, it was so hard… How was I going to tell Big Bro I can't deal with him anymore? I got back to Philly and before I could even shower Big Bro was calling my phone. He wanted me to meet him at "the office," the strip club, for dinner. I was so nervous, but I got dressed and headed over there. Three double shots of tequila and a bowl of clams later, and I was sitting at the table by myself. Big Bro went upstairs to have a "meeting." I was so drunk I had to use the bathroom, and as I'm making my way to the ladies room I see Big Bro walking towards me. Midway to the bathroom entrance, I see him standing with a group of guys he's talking loud moving his hands around. As I got closer, I realized one of the guys happen to be Bee. *Shit*, I was about to pee on myself. What the fuck was Bee doing there? I rushed past them with my head down, and I stayed in the bathroom for what seemed like forever. Standing in the stall and thinking what the hell was I going to say to either of them. Yea Bee knew about me and Big Bro, but Big Bro didn't know how Bee felt about us dealing, let alone that I just sucked his dick three hours ago.

I gathered myself and walked out the bathroom. There they were still talking. I walked right up in between them and said "hi" in the dumbest voice ever.

All the guys spoke,

Bee looked at me. "What's up, fam?" he had this sneaky ass grin on his face.

I said "hey" in the same dumb voice.

Big Bro asked if he wanted a shot.

Bee answered with a simple, "Yeah."

That lightened the mood. I ordered us all another shot.

The rest of the night went smooth. Bee stayed at the bar for about thirty minutes the other guys went their own way. Bee then proceeded to entertain or be entertained by the strippers. He texted me a few times just to talk shit. He even suggested I let this be the last night I spent time with Big Bro. I responded that I would break it off. I really couldn't understand why Bee was taking it so personal. I wasn't prepared to break things off. I liked Big Bro. He was fun and we enjoyed each other.

I left with Big Bro, and we stayed at the hotel. Still no sex. I couldn't muster up the strength to break shit off. I didn't even mention it. We were so drunk from the shots of Patron that we passed out as soon as we hit the bed. I woke up to over sixteen text from Bee. I just didn't get why he was being such a hater. I lied and told him I was home and that I had ended things last night. I was planning to keep things a secret for as long as I could. Shit, I'm grown and Bee was my closest male friend, but he wasn't paying my bills. I wasn't going to take money out my own pocket. I needed Bee for the sex. I just had to be careful.

June 2009

It had been about a year and nothing really changed. Big Bro and I didn't really have a sexual relationship. We went out a lot, ate, drank, and got in these stupid fights almost every week. He was never physically abusive, but he could make a bitch cry with his words. Not me, though. I paid his ass no mind. I knew his yelling was just part of his overbearing personality. He knew he wasn't scaring me. He liked being around me. I could tell I was a trophy for him. He felt good having a young girl on his arm. I had been on his hip for so many events, his birthday, his close friends' birthdays. Hell, I even attended a few family events with him. The sex thing really bothered me, but he was giving me money and buying me shit, so after a while I didn't even care. I would suck his dick from time to time. I was starting to feel bad that he wasn't getting none of my juicy box.

Like a fool I was still having sex with Bee. It wasn't all the time since he was constantly in and out of town. He started going over to the west coast, so I wouldn't see him too often. Bee asked me if I could come over to Phoenix to visit him for a few days. I agreed.

***

Arizona was so hot. When I got off the plane, the temperature on my phone read 104 degrees. Bee pulled up to get me in a brand-new Mercedes. He drove me all around, showing me his new city, all the hot spots, and all the malls (he knew how much I loved to shop). We ended up at his townhouse. It was a beautiful bi-level with three bedrooms in a gated community with a pool, gym, and tennis court on the property. It was perfect. I drifted off thinking of what my life would be like if I lived there. It was totally different form Philly. I was starting to realize why Bee liked it over here so much.

We were going out, so I needed to shower, but before I got in the shower Bee came in and started telling me his friend is on her way. She was some mixed chick from out there. He tells me that he's been using her to get cars and stuff in her name. I asked if he fucked her, and he just looked at me, which meant yes. He told her I was his ex-wife. I came in town for my birthday, and he wanted to show me a good time. I was pissed! Here I was way across the country and again about to play girlfriend number two. I didn't say a word, just walked in the bathroom and started getting ready.

I put on the best outfit I packed. I wasn't about to let some new bitch look better than me. I walked in to the living room and there she was. As soon as I walked down the steps, she ran towards me, "You're beautiful!" she said with this big smile on her face.

"Me?" I replied, questioning her honesty.

"Yes," she answered as she handed me a drink. "I'm Lina," she said as I grabbed the cup. "Bee has told me all about you."

Bee stands in between us and wraps his arm around my waist, "Y'all ready to go?"

He told us we were going to some club in downtown Phoenix, but first we were going to the strip club to pregame. I was excited since this was my first night out here and Lina seemed cool. I was just ready to hear some good music and unwind a little bit.

We arrived at the strip club, and Bee knows everybody. This really was his second home. We got a little section and ordered a few bottles. After a few drinks, Lina was all over Bee, grabbing his arm, dancing on him. She even gave him a lap dance. It was a mess. I could tell she was the type of chick that couldn't hold her liquor. We stayed at the strip club for a few hours and then headed to the club. It had to be 90 degrees even though it as after eleven. By now my hair is a mess and my tight dress is sticking to me like a glove. I ended up pulling my hair into a ponytail before we walked inside. This club had a really nice indoor-outdoor setup, and it was packed. Bee had a few of his guy friends meet us there too, so our trio had grown to a crew of six. We got bottle service, and they sat us at this table right in the middle of the party. Lina's intoxication decreased a little, but she was still all over Bee. I can't front. The shit was annoying as hell. It was like torture watching her enjoy him. I had known Bee forever, and I just never understood why I wasn't his choice. I mean I knew he fucked with me. He trusted me and would do anything for me. He just never made me his girl. I was in my feelings heavy. So I decided to dip off and check the club out by myself. I reached the dance floor and the DJ started playing Jay-Z's "Big Pimping." How ironic. I loved Hov, so I was jamming in my own little world when all of a sudden I felt someone behind me. I turn around and it was Lina. This bitch just won't quit. I wasn't tripping. I started dancing with her, throwing my hips around and bouncing my ass. She was loving it, and my drinks were kicking in, so I was in a great mood. We musta danced for five songs straight. I was dripping in sweat, and Lina's crazy ass wanted to dance some more. But I needed to sit my ass down for a few. Bee was at the table talking to his friend Mike when we walked up on them. Mike was cute as shit, tall, brown skin with nice wavy hair. Shit, Bee had better be lucky I wasn't a ho no more…

"What y'all doing ?" Bee asked.

"Ya bitch is a dancing machine," I said, wiping the sweat off my face.

Bee laughed.

I sat down right beside Mike. Damn, this nigga even smelled good. By now it was a little after two and Bee asked if he wanted to get some food. I was ready to eat, so I had to go fetch Lina from the dance floor. She somehow managed to get back out there after I sat down.

"Come on, girl. Bee's ready to go," I said as I grabbed her by the arm.

She walked back, stumbling a little bit, and we made eye contact with the boys. We all proceeded to the exit. We ended up at a diner. Everybody was starving. Lina was sitting right next to me, and I made her get a ginger ale. I was starting to feel like her babysitter, but I knew from earlier she couldn't hold her liquor. She wore a white crop top and some denim cut off shorts. Her body was really nice with small west coast tits and thick thighs. She didn't really have much of an ass, but she had long ass hair down her back and these full ass lips and dark eyes. She was sexy. I couldn't deny that. Midway through our late-night dinner, her hand was up my dress. I wasn't wearing panties, because I never do, and she was playing with my clit in between taking bites of her burger, and I was enjoying it. I don't know if Bee knew at this point. For all I knew, he was telling her to do it. He knew I was a nasty bitch, and somehow Lina got the memo. I don't know how I kept a straight face, but I maintained my composure for the entire meal. We got up to leave and a small amount of my juice leaked on the diner floor. *Shit,* I'm thinking to myself. But there was nothing I could do about it. I had been holding it in for about an hour.

Bee said goodnight to his friends, and we all got in the car and headed back to the house. I was sitting in the front seat. Lina sat right behind me and was rubbing my shoulders the whole ride. Once we got in the house, I ran straight to the bathroom. I needed to collect my thoughts because I knew what was about to happen. I came back into the living room, and there was Lina naked on the sofa. This bitch looked like a goddess, her long dark hair pushed to one side and her boobs perfect and firm with cocoa brown areolas. My pussy dripped. I wanted to run over there and suck on her whole body, but I didn't. I took my time and walked towards her. I asked where Bee was, and she said she didn't know."

I want you," she said. My mouth dropped. I was sure Bee had put her up to all this, but at this point I was horny as hell and couldn't resist. Lina started kissing me. Her mouth was wet and juicy, her lips soft like mine. She must have been feeling me too because the kissing session lasted like five minutes. I was still wearing my dress when she pushed my body back onto the couch and proceeded to kiss my inner thigh. She knew what she was doing too. She made her way to my thick clit and rotated her tongue across it, first going really slow but then she moved it faster and faster. I was moaning so loud I know Bee could hear me wherever he was. She came up for air and released some of my juices into my mouth. I sat up just enough to reach her boobs and started making circles around her nipples. I gestured for her to put her pussy on my face. Her little body fit perfectly in my arms. Lina rode my face like a pro, and her pussy tasted so pure. It was sopping wet as I massaged her clit slowly, and I could taste her climax. All of a sudden, Bee came up behind her and grabbed a fist full of her hair.

"Y'all cheating on me?" I heard him say.

I had a mouth full of pussy, so I didn't say a word. Lina moaned out a no. Bees took his hands and pulled my dress up more and entered me. It felt like a ton of bricks. He was grabbing my waist, pulling me closer with each stroke, and I tried to maintain my rhythm as I'm feasting on Lina. The harder he pounds me, the harder I suck. I'm about to lose control when Bee flips me over. Lina damn near flew off the couch. He inserted his dick back inside me, gripping my ass really tight as his strokes become more and more aggressive. It felt so good my river was about to flow, and I screamed, "I'm about to squirt!" He flipped me over and plucked my clit a few times. As a waterfall exits my body, Lina jumps up and catches my juice in her mouth. Bee sucked the juice right out her mouth, and my body was out of control as I continued squirting more than I ever had. Finally, the waterworks stopped, and I sat up. Both Bee and Lina were drenched in my juices on the living room floor. The floor was soaked. The couch soaked too. I stepped over them and headed upstairs. I made it to the bedroom, lay down, and pull the covers over my head and pass out.

Talk about the walk of shame. The next morning I didn't wanna get up. I walked into the living room. Thank god Lina was gone. Bee was standing the kitchen naked, drinking some orange juice. I didn't want to see him either, but I had created this anything goes relationship, and I had to face the music.

"Last night was bangin," he said with a smile.

I just nodded my head in agreement, "What we doing today?" I asked him trying to change the subject.

"We about to roll out. I got some shit to do, so go get dressed."

I got dressed, and Bee and I headed out for the day. We did basic stuff. Ate, he got a haircut, and we went to the mall. Finally, something I wanted to do. I ended up getting a few pair of shoes and this cute bracelet. Bee was generous, and he knew I wasn't trying to hear him telling me no. I spent a few more days in Arizona. Me and Bee fucked a few more times, alone! Lina came by to see me before I left. She was in love with me (her words). We exchanged numbers, and I headed back to Philly.

On the plane ride home, I started feeling really guilty. I had created this crazy life for myself full of sexual episodes and cash. I was spending time with a few different guys, but there was nothing there. No feelings, well except for Bee. I actually loved him, and I knew we would never be together because of his baby mom and the fact that I allowed our relationship to go way too far. I should have set some boundaries. I should have been able to tell him no. But it was too late. I was the fun girl, the party starter. I didn't want to play those roles anymore. It was something about this trip that made me feel like I deserved better. I could be giving this good pussy to my own man, someone who really cared about me. Right?

February 2010

"Can you believe I haven't had sex in a whole six months?"

"You a whole fucking liar!" Nia was looking at me like I had three heads.

"Bitch, no lie! I'm trying to get me a boyfriend."

Those words came out my mouth in slow motion. I was actually telling the truth. It had been a little over six months with no sex. I had not heard from Bee. Big Bro was acting funny, and I was trying to find some peace.

I came to see Nia to hear all about this new man she was dealing with. Nia had recently become Muslim, and her ass had already been married twice. This new one, she said, was the one. I was happy for her but secretly I wasn't feeling the "new Nia." She was allowing men to manipulate her, moving them into her house, letting them tell her what to do, what to wear. I wasn't feeling it at all. But Nia was my girl, and I wasn't going to say all that to her. I just listened. I mean, there was a good side to it. She was faithful to these losers, and she seemed happy. Seeing her like this made me hopeful that I could find somebody too, but I wasn't about to cover my face and move some broke nigga in my house to get it. After I ate a bunch of halal food, I was ready for a nap. I slept on Nia's couch for like hour before her new husband called and said he was on his way home She damn near dragged me out the front door.

On the way home, I got a call from one of my friends telling me she wanted me to meet this guy. She had introduced me to a few guys in the past, and they turned out okay, so I agreed. She told me he had a couple dollars. He was from West Philly. I usually stayed away from guys from my part of the city. I told her about my boyfriend search and how I wasn't trying to just be fucking nobody right now. After hearing all about him, I figured it was at least worth a date, so I told her to give him my number.

He called me right away, and we agreed to meet up the following night down old city at this spot called Blue Martini. Originally, I was going to drive there myself, but he insisted that he pick me up. I made him come get me from my grandmother's house. I didn't know him yet, and I didn't want him knowing where I lived.

A navy Mercedes CLS pulled up blasting music. I walked down the steps, waving my hands in the air and trying to get his attention, so he could turn the music down. *Straight hood*, I'm thinking to myself as I get closer to the car. I open the door and get smacked in the face by a cloud of smoke. He doesn't even turn his head to acknowledge me. I waved the weed smoke out my face and attempted to get comfy in my seat. I reached forward to turn the music down.

"Well hi," I was honestly a little upset, but I played it off and rubbed his hand as I spoke to him. "Mal, right?" He nodded his head and turned the music back up a little bit.

"We going to Blue Martini, right?" I asked.

"Yea, but I wanna make a stop first. Is that cool?"

"Yeah, you good," I replied while staring out the window. I was almost mad at myself for agreeing to come on this date.

It had been a long time since I went out with a "street nigga," especially from Philly. Mal was super dark skinned and thin built. I couldn't wait to get out the car so I could see how tall he was. He wore Creed cologne; I knew that smell anywhere. He had a few diamond bracelets on and a nice watch, but I could tell he was still in the streets because he was driving so fast. We pull up to Sables, this hood strip club I had never been inside but was in West Philly, so I knew all about it. He stepped out the car, and I noticed he walked with a little limp. He wasn't too short, so that was good. We might be around the same height, but of course, I was wearing heels.

Inside, I'm hit with the musty scent of bath and body works spray and stripper pole. It was a distinct smell only available in the hood clubs.

Mal was the man in Sables. Both the bartenders rushed to take his order. That was until they realized he wasn't alone. They saw me place my Gucci clutch on the bar and sit beside him. One of them turned the other way and the other one cut her eye at me and proceeded to take the order. He ordered us both double shots of Henny. I didn't really drink brown, but I took it. I wasn't going to be difficult. I really didn't even want to be sitting in here, but I was trying to relax and see how this night was going to end up. Two more shots in and finally this light skinned, heavy set guy came in and greeted Mal. They dipped off to talk. He spent about fifteen minutes taking to guy and then tapped me on the shoulder to let me know it was time to go. *Thank god*, I was thinking to myself. I had been looking at 22-year-old girls shaking they infant size asses for long enough. Not one of the girls working turned me on. I barely saw them getting tips. This was the saddest strip club I had ever been in. We got back in the car and he blasted the music all the way downtown.

Blue Martini was a chill little spot. The food was always good, and they had really good drinks. We sat in a small booth towards the back of the restaurant and finally I felt like I could get a good look at him. Mal started talking, and I noticed a missing tooth. For some reason it didn't bother me. I guess he made up for it in diamonds. We talked about everything from music to sports. We had some of the same favorite basketball teams, and we liked some of the same music. Mal wasn't as hood as he seemed. He was actually a little smart, funny too, and slowly making me see why my girlfriend thought we would might along. I wanted to ask him what he did for money, but I was convinced he was a drug dealer, so I didn't say anything. Mal dropped me back off at my grandmother's house around one in the morning. I gave him a hug and told him I would call him later. He turned his music up super loud and pulled off. I headed home in my own car.

It was barely nine in the morning when my phone started ringing. "You up? I'm outside," I hear Mal yelling in the phone.

"Up? Outside? What!?"

"Yeah, I'm outside, babe. Get up."

I was thinking there ain't no way he's outside. He didn't even know where I lived. I jumped outta bed and looked out the window. I'd be damned. This nigga was outside.

"I'm sleep, Mal, and what you doing here?"

"I want you to take a ride with me," he said.

"Alright, you gotta give me twenty minutes."

I jumped in the shower and threw on a Juicy tracksuit. Thank god my hair was done from the night before. It was a little chilly out, so I grabbed my coat and walked out the door.

"How you know where I live!?" I'm yelling before I even sat completely in my seat.

"Don't worry about it," Mal said as he sped down my block.

"Where we going?"

"I just gotta make a run."

"What you mean you gotta make a run? Mal, I'm not riding around with you busting traps. What type of bitch you think I am?"

"Bussing a trap?" He looks at me with this dumbass look on his face. "I don't sell drugs!"

"Oh, you don't?"

Mal started telling me about his hustle. He ran a very lucrative instant credit business. He had workers that used profiles to get instant credit from department stores, jewelry stores, electronic stores, and they even did bank scams. Mal was the ring leader and had a crew working for him in three different parts of the city. He rarely got his hands dirty, but he did follow the workers while they went on bank runs. Mal told me he cashed out at about 20k a week depending on what they were able to get. We pulled up to a gas station on Greys Ferry Avenue. Mal grabbed an envelope from the dash and got out the car. A black jeep pulled up, he handed it to the driver, he got back in the car, waited for the jeep to get out of sight, and then we pulled off. He told me we were headed to North Philly. We met his friend right off of Ridge Ave. I'll call him Talk.

Talk got in the backseat and started talking business. I was surprised because he didn't know me. Most guys wouldn't talk so freely in front of a stranger, but he did. He told Mal he needed some more profiles, and a few more D's. I later found out that "D's" were code word for ID's, and in order for the work to get done each runner needed a fake ID that displayed the name of the person's identity they stole. In that same conversation with Talk, I learned what was in the envelope Mal dropped off earlier that morning. The envelope was filled with seconds, AKA credit cards, that were made for the runners to use as a second form of ID. Talk went on and on about how they needed to get the seconds cheaper. The supplier they had currently was charging $200 each, and that was money that came directly out of the profit. I realized that Talk was Mal's business partner. Mal was responsible for getting the workers the ID's and seconds. Talk had a chick that worked in healthcare, so she was able to pull profiles for them. Talk also had the connect for the rental cars. The workers only used rental cars when they worked. It was less of a chance for them to get caught that way. Talk would rent three different cars each week. The workers would rotate vehicles, and the cars would get switched out weekly to avoid anybody catching on. I hadn't been with Mal for 48 hours yet and knew enough to put him in jail for the rest of his life. I was mind blown by the fact that he was saying all of this in front of me. I was listening very carefully to everything they were saying though. It was fascinating that these two guys from the hood were running a million-dollar operation and their office was the inside of a Benz.

After the meeting with Talk, Mal asked if I was hungry. We headed to Honeys, this cute breakfast spot in Northern Liberties. Over breakfast, I asked Mal about his limp. He told me he had recently been in a motorcycle accident and was told he'd never walk again. Mal said he broke both his legs and was in the hospital for weeks. He couldn't even wash on his own. The doctors told him he would most likely be in rehab for 12 to 24 months. During his first week in the rehab he had a nurse help him wipe his ass. That was the day he got up and walked. Mal said he felt helpless and embarrassed. He didn't want a stranger cleaning him. He had managed to walk just weeks after a near fatal crash. The medical staff couldn't believe it. And I couldn't either. The accident was only six months ago. Hearing Mal tell that story made me like him even more. He was strong, and he was resilient. This nigga was like a real life superhero.

I think that was the day Mal won me over because three weeks had past, and I was with him every single day. We had a daily routine. Mal would pick me up around eight in the morning, we would meet up with Talk and go to breakfast. Most days we would wait around for the first drop of the day, cash the workers out, and go shopping. If it was a slow day we would go to the movies or just chill in the house. My house. I was never the type to have a bunch of different guys in my house. Mal had this charming side to him. Even though he was super hood, he knew how to get what he wanted.

Our first time fucking wasn't much to talk about. Mal got us hotel room. He had taken me out, and we both got super drunk. We were over Cherry Hill, New Jersey, and I didn't want to chance driving over the bridge tipsy. Mal jumped right out his jeans and onto the bed. I was so drunk, I think I went straight to pee. I see him spread out across the bed with his skinny black legs spread wide open. For some reason, as much as I was starting to like Mal, I wasn't sexually attracted to him, but I played it off, jumped in bed next to him, and to proceeded to pull his boxers down. His dick was a nice size, maybe eight or nine inches. He had this bump in his dick he later told me was some kind of piercing that was supposed to give his partner extra pleasure. (I didn't believe him. I still don't know what the fuck that was.) I had never seen a dick with a bump, so I pulled a condom off the dresser and sucked his dick fully protected. I went wild on his dick. My mouth was so wet, and I created large pools of saliva in that bed. Mal was screaming he was about to cum, so I stopped and hopped on top and started to ride him. He grabbed my ass really tight, making it hard for me to bounce up and down on him. He pulled my body really close and released the loudest moan I had ever heard. Mal shot a huge load into the condom. When I jumped off his dick and took the condom off, he was still cumming. He stood up and shot the rest of his load on my stomach. We both rolled over and fell asleep.

All of our sexual encounters went pretty much the same way… quick! He came in minutes each time, leaving me to pleasure myself so that I could cum too. This one night after a quickie, Mal asked if I had a DVD player. I went in my closet and found one, and he hooked it up to the TV and told me he would be right back. He went out to the car and returned with a black bag full of movies. Porno movies. Mal told me he loved porn. He especially liked watching gang bangs. It was the reason he would cum so fast. He was watching porn all day, so when it was time to get some pussy, he was already rear a climax. We watched a few movies together that night and had a few quicker sex sessions before we went to sleep. I was so curious about his porn addiction that I started watching the movies when I was alone. Before now, I had never really been into porn. I did like watching girl on girl. Mal had a few movies that were strictly girl on girl, and I began watching them more and more to get myself off. At the end of one of the videos it was a preview of a movie called Tranny Surprise. All I saw was a pretty bitch with a huge dick. My mouth dropped and my pussy got super wet. I ended up watching the four-minute preview a half dozen times, each time being more and more turned on. I don't know why I was so aroused. My body would tense up and I would squirt all over my own hand. The image of a female pounding her dick inside a man turned me on. Within days I was out buying my own movies. I secretly started watching tranny porn daily. It became my pre-game for sex. I didn't feel bad about it either.

Mal was one of the first guys I wasn't having mind-blowing sex with. I liked him a lot, but we just didn't have chemistry. I should have left him alone in the beginning, but he was stuck to me like glue. He was funny, and we always had a good time together. If I could get off during my porn sessions, his mediocre sex wasn't too bad. We weren't having sex on a consistent basis. We would fuck a few times a month if that. He was always chasing a dollar. I wasn't complaining because with his "job" came a lot of gifts. Watches, diamond earrings, bracelets, designer shoes, and weekly shopping sprees.

I'm sure you know that with all this good came some bad.

Mal was always drunk. We had been together only about six months and he had already had three DUIs. His drinking and drug use started to take over his life. Mal was addicted to codeine, AKA syrup. He would be so high that at night time he would break out in a cold sweat. His body would shake. I hated sleeping next to him during his episodes. He also had a bad temper. He would cuss people out for no reason. He hated waiting, and he hated hearing someone tell him no. He was the boss, and if it weren't for him, no one would eat. He made sure he let the workers know that every single day. I used to try to get him to calm down, but he never listened. I didn't like hearing him disrespecting and yelling at his workers, especially the females. He was a totally different person when he was high. I knew not to say much when he was. I preferred the sober Mal. He stayed out most nights, so I usually got the better version of him when we were together.

Mal always made sure I had something nice to drive. He rented me this Benz truck for the month. It was one of the nicest cars I had ever drove. I was riding around the city, spending money on dumb stuff. His money was coming in so fast it didn't matter. I was getting an allowance of like $1,200 a day, plus he would give me gift cards to spend in certain stores. I was having the time of my life. One day Mal asked me to go meet up with Talk. I didn't really want to go, but he was in D.C. working, so I didn't have a choice. I pulled up and Talk was standing in the middle of the street. He gestured for me to pull into this garage. I pulled in, and he told me to get out the car. Talk handed me a bag full of money, told me to go to 5th Street to a cell phone store, ask for Donny, and hand Donny the bag.

"Donny will tell you to pull around the side of the building. He's going to put a box in the trunk of your car. Take the box home and put it up. Mal will know what to do with it."

"Okay," I agreed with his orders, but the whole time I'm thinking *what the fuck!? Mal got me out here working for him.*

I drove straight down 5th Street, saw the cell phone store on the corner, and pulled on the side of the building. Walking in, I was shocked to see a Chinese guy behind the counter. I went up to the desk and asked for Danny. He looked me up and down said something in his language. An older Chinese man came out from the back, looked down at the Hugo Boss bag in my hand, and walked to the counter.

"Go round back."

I barely understood what he was saying, but walked out the store and headed to the back. My car was already parked on the side, so I didn't have to move it. Danny came out the side door and handed me a small brown box. I handed him the bag. I got in the car and pulled off. I drove straight home. Once I got in my bedroom, I opened the box. It was full of credit cards. Each card had a different name on it. It also had a note that read: "$500 on each. You have 48 hours to use once its swiped."

I couldn't believe the Chinese made the seconds! It was mind blowing. I put the box in the closet and called Mal. I let him know I had met Talk and picked the box up from 5th Street. He told me to take two cards for myself and spend them today. He said he would be back in the morning to work. Mal came home and did just that. We went straight to work. He cleared about 90k that week. Of course, him and Talk split it, and the workers had to be paid, but I was looking at 35 thousand dollars cash on my bed, and it was a beautiful sight.

Winter 2011

It was almost Christmas Mal had hit a big lick. He had been running around with these new guys from DC. They did a wire transfer for 95 thousand, it was three of them so each one walked away with over 20k Mal was excited because Jay-Z and Kanye West were on tour. Mal said I could pick two cities to see the concert in, and he said he wanted to take me to this comedy show. He gave ten thousand to get all the tickets and to go shopping he also gave me five thousand more to pay all his bills. The rest of the money he put in the safe.

I had the best Christmas that year. Mal spoiled me, and even though he was Muslim and not even supposed to celebrate, he made sure I was happy. The comedy show was the night before New Year's Eve. I had forgot about it and planned to hang out with my girlfriends that night. Mal came in the house all dressed up and reminded me. I called my girls and told them I would come over after the show.

We arrived at the venue a little early. Mal knew a few of the comedians personally, so we had backstage access. We sat back there and talked with his friends. This guy I used to date walked into the green room. We said a few words to each other. Mal came over and asked who I was talking to, so I told him who he was. His whole attitude changed. He was so upset that I spoke to the guy.

"Don't talk to no niggaz when you out with me!" he was yelling all in my face.

I was embarrassed, so I walked out of the green room and into the arena. I needed to get a drink because Mal was tripping. As I paid for my drink, I heard Mal yelling and screaming. "Don't walk away from me, bitch!" He was yelling through the crowd.

I turned the other way. I didn't want anybody to know he was talking to me. He caught up with me and grabbed my arm, "You hear me?" He was still yelling.

"Yes, I hear you." I tell him that I'm going to leave. He was clearly intoxicated, and I just wanted to go home. I walked out of the venue and started walking up the street. I wasn't too far from home, and even though it was almost January, the weather was nice. As I was walking up the street, I called my girlfriend and told her I was going to show up at the party early. I was so annoyed and just wanted to get away from Mal. I reached the top of the block when I see this car pull up. It was Mal. He jumped out the car and ran towards me.

"Didn't I say don't walk away from me!?" he was yelling again.

I tried to get some words out, but before I could speak he slapped me. I grabbed my mouth as it starts bleeding. I tried to gather myself, but he started punching me in my face. Mal was hitting me so hard I fell on the ground. He stood over me and kicked me in my chest. He kept kicking me so hard I balled up into the fetal position trying to protect myself. I put my hand over my face. I felt like three people were attacking me at the same time. The whole time, I was just praying he stopped. What felt like forever was only about two minutes. Mal beat me down, jumped in his car, and pulled off. I lifted my face up in time to see him pull off. My stomach was in so much pain and my face felt like it was falling off. My hands were full of blood, my shirt was torn, my heel was broken. I sat on the corner trying to figure out what I was going to do. About five minutes later, Mal pulled back up he dragged my lifeless body into the backseat of the car. I was crying and bleeding like I had just got shot.

"I'm sorry, shit. I'm sorry," Mal was hitting the dashboard, yelling and screaming. "What the fuck did I do?" he's asked. I couldn't even talk. My mouth was on fire. I was praying my teeth weren't knocked out.

Mal pulled up to a hotel and told me to stay in the car. I felt like I was dying on the backseat. He came back and handed me a tee shirt. "Put this over your face."

I covered my face and made it up to the room. I laid on the bed, still bleeding out. I was so scared to look in the mirror. I must have fallen asleep, and when I finally woke up, I went into the bathroom and couldn't believe what I saw. My face was bruised and swollen. I had dried up blood coming from my left eye and my mouth. My chest and shoulders were black and blue. I felt like I had just been run over by a bus. I had never been hit by any man before. Mal had just beat me and left me in a hotel to deal with it on my own. I felt so stupid. Men don't abuse me. I wasn't a weak bitch. I had never let myself get caught up like this before. Who was I becoming? So much was going on in my mind. I always said that I would never let a man abuse me. How could this happen? Was I blinded by the money and gifts? All this was my fault. I let my guard down. I gave him the upper hand, and my face was proof that I had allowed this relationship to spin way out of control. All I could do was wash my face and lay in bed. I couldn't go home. I was too embarrassed to tell my friends. I drifted back off to sleep, praying I would have a plan by the time I woke back up.

My father had been in prison all my life, he was convicted of a few murders and was never coming home. My sister and I used to visit when we were younger. We would go to the prison on family day. They had games and food for the kids to play. As we got older, we stopped the visits, but he would call from time to time to check on us. My mom tried to keep the lines of commination open, but he was crazy for real, and it always ended up being some drama.

I had a good relationship with his mother. I even lived with her for a little while. She was cool down to earth, and she didn't take no shit. My dad started writing my sister and I separately. He would ask about school, and once we were teenagers, he was starting to ask us about boys. It didn't bother me at first because I figured he was just trying to get to know his girls. One day I got a letter from him and the envelope was really thick. In the letter he said he wanted to know if I started having sex yet. He went on to say he always knew I would grow up to be a whore. He told me I needed to send photos of myself in swimwear or sexy lingerie and if I didn't, he would have someone kill my mom. I couldn't believe what I was reading. This was my dad asking to see my body. He also requested that I tell him in detail about my sexual encounters. I was so scared I didn't know what to do, so at first, I ignored his request.

About a month later he called the house and asked to speak to me. I got on the phone, and he started talking to me in a low tone. He asked if I got his letter. Scared of what might happen, I said yes. He told me I had a week to respond or he would send the shooter. He knew where my mom worked, and since he was in jail for murder, I believed him. I started writing him about sex. Half the stuff I was making up. He stopped requesting pictures, so I never sent them. His letters kept coming and his requests got more and more explicit. I couldn't believe my dad was doing this.

After a few years passed, he started requesting the photos again. He wanted to see my pink pussy (his words). He even tried to get me to come visit him. I made up a ton of excuses and never went to that prison. But the abuse never stooped. He harassed me until I was about twenty-two years old. He would call and make me moan on the phone. He would disrespect me and tell me I was a whore. He would make me describe how I sucked dick. It was awful. I felt like shit. I mean, my father was treating me like a sex object. I was so scared to tell anyone about it. He would threaten my life and the life of my family. I was a child and he made me feel useless and dirty. I couldn't take it anymore, so I finally told my mom. She didn't believe me at first, but my sister did. I got up enough courage to write a letter to the warden telling them that I had been being harassed. The letters stopped, but the pain was permanent.

I went through my life feeling like all men wanted from me was sex. I didn't trust anyone, not even my own mother. He had managed to make me feel useless and disgusting through words. I hated myself, and sex became my revenge. I wanted men to beg for me. I wanted somebody to pay.

I don't think I ever fully recovered from the mental and sexual abuse I had been through. I told myself that I would never allow a man to make me feel like that again. I was so young when it all started. As an adult I had control. I had the power to say yes or no. I was determined not to ever get caught slipping again.

I stayed in the hotel alone for almost two days. Mal came back with food and a black bag from Shine Jewelers. I didn't even care what was in the bag. I had time to play back the whole year we had spent together, all the toxic behavior I allowed. All the crimes I watched him commit, the drugs and drinking, the yelling and screaming. I had enough. He couldn't even look me in the face. He kept his head down while he talked to me. I begged him to look at my face, "Look at what you did!" I yelled over and over.

He wouldn't look. He kept saying how sorry he was and how it would never happen again. He had the nerve to say I pushed him too far, and that I should have listened to him. I knew how crazy he was. He was right. I did know how crazy he was, but for some reason I never thought he would do something like this to me. I couldn't find the words to say what I was thinking. I listened to Mal's reasons for beating my ass over breakfast while I could hardly eat because my lip was split open. This whole conversation was pointless. I had already made my mind up. I was done with Mal. I had an exit plan. I just needed a little bit more time to heal.

He left after he ate, told me he had to get with Talk and put something in motion for the day. I asked if he could extend the room another night and get me some big sunglasses and some clothes. I wasn't ready to come outside just yet. My face was still really swollen, and my eyes had turned black from all the punching. He agreed and walked out the door.

Two days later...

I was finally home. Nobody was there, so it was a perfect opportunity for me to put my plan in motion. I didn't want anybody to know that Mal had beat my ass, so I came up with a plan to explain why my face was tore up. I went down my basement and broke the banister. I brought my broken shoe and heel to put at the bottom of the steps. I called my mom and sister and told them I had fallen down the steps and Mal was taking me to the ER. I don't know if they believed me, but that was all I could think of. Once I staged my fall, I went upstairs and packed up all Mal's stuff. He had a ton of clothes and sneakers at my house. He had also brought over this big screen T.V and a ton of porno movies. I packed everything into the truck. Mal had just got a brand-new caddy truck, but I was the one driving it most of the time. He stayed in the rental since he worked during the day. I drove the truck to his mother's house, parked it, and put the keys in her mail box. I called a cab to pick me up and take me back home. As I headed home my stomach was in knots. I felt so ashamed. I was fighting back tears through the whole ride. I had been so pressed to be in just one real relationship that I went for the first one. I felt so stupid. It was time for me to get myself together. I didn't even know who I was anymore.

By late afternoon he was blowing my phone up. I'm sure by now his mom had called and he knew all his shit was at her house. I ignored his calls for the whole day. By 9pm he was at my front door. I wouldn't let him in. He kept begging me to, but I wasn't budging. He slid the Shine Jewelers bag in my mail slot and asked me to please give him another chance. I took the bag, turned all the downstairs lights off, and went to bed.

The begging went on for another week. He called me nonstop day and night. I didn't want to hear nothing he had to say. After a few weeks passed I finally called him back. My face was almost back to normal, and I had to get a few things off my chest.

Of course, he answered on the first ring. "Mal, listen, I know you said you're sorry, and I believe you are, but this hitting shit is not cool."

I went on to tell him I didn't think it was a good idea for us to continue, that I would never look at him the same and couldn't trust him. He said he changed, and he was so sorry, but I knew I couldn't let him back in my life. I ended the conversation by saying we would always be friends. I told him I would always be there for him, but we just couldn't be together. That was one of the hardest conversations I ever had, but it was necessary.

Everybody wanted to know where Mal was. All my friends and family had grown to like him. I told them we broke up, still too embarrassed to say he hit me. I made up some bullshit story about him cheating and not being able to trust him. After a month or so the questions stopped. Mal wasn't calling as much anymore either. He would text me here and there just to say hi. He called me one day and told me he was relocating to Atlanta, which was something we had talked about when we were together. I told him I thought it was a good idea. A fresh start and he was so flashy he would fit right in.

It was so hard rebuilding my confidence after the abuse. I never verbalized what I was going through. From the outside looking in I know nobody could tell, but I was dying inside. I felt so ugly and so stupid. I was trying everything to feel like the old me again. I realized that I was never going to be the same. Mal, like so many other men, had taken something form me. I was constantly being stripped of my pride and self-worth. Each time I left a man alone I was also removing a layer of myself. This had been the most extreme situation I had endured, and it felt like it. All the money and gifts didn't mean anything. Every time I looked in the mirror I saw my beat down face. That night played in my head over and over. I knew this was going to be hard to get through.

Finally, I was ready to clean up my room. I had stuff everywhere from the day I packed up all of Mal's stuff. I wanted to rearrange my bedroom furniture. I went to Bed, Bath, and Beyond and bought a pretty new comforter set, a new rug, and some cute little bedroom accessories. I was trying to erase any memory of him. As I moved shoeboxes around in the closet, a small black safe fell out. *Shit.* I forgot to give Mal his safe. I grabbed it and ran to the drawer to find the paper with the code. I opened the safe, and inside was six grand. I couldn't believe it. I closed and put the safe under my bed. I told myself I wouldn't touch the money for a month and if Mal didn't call me about it, it was mine. I also found that inside that Shine Jewelers bag was a diamond key necklace. It was beautiful, and I put it right on. I figured after all he put me through I deserved some diamonds. That night I had the best sleep ever. My space was clean, and I had gotten rid of everything that reminded me of Mal, except the cash.

Three months later...

"God really must love me!" I'm telling Nia as I hang up the phone.

I had just found out Mal got picked up by the feds. They say he was a person of interest since 2009, and they raided his apartment in Atlanta and found all kinds of shit in there. *Wow!* I couldn't believe it! I was just with this man every day for over a year. I was starting to feel real lucky, but sad for him at the same time. I was sure somebody set him up, probably Talk, who was always running his mouth. I had come up with a hundred different scenarios since I heard the bad news. I was also a little nervous; if they had been watching him since 09, they had to know about me. I was praying the feds weren't coming for me next.

I dodged a bullet. A few weeks went by and no feds. Mal had gotten in touch with me and explained I had nothing to worry about. He said he had a lawyer and he was good. He didn't mention anything about the safe, so it was as good as mine. And I couldn't have been happier. It was like a huge weight lifted off my shoulders. I was finally free of Mal for good.

2014

"We are all addicted to this shit, Nia. Just because your boring ass wants to be a housewife, some of us are still sexy and single."

I wasted my breath trying to tell Nia about Instagram. I was loving this new app. It's just a picture posting app. You post a pic and people like them. You can get followers from all over the world. I was having a good time posting, and I liked seeing what people from other places were wearing and doing. Nia didn't even have a camera phone. She was still on her Muslim shit and newly married to husband number four. She was still one of my best friends and one of the only people I could trust.

My sex life was basically non-existent. I was trying to focus on me. Plus, I started traveling a lot more. I had a few new guy friends in L.A. and was flying out there every chance I got. Philly was starting to be so boring with the same people, same clubs, and lately, so much killing. It was hard trying to date. Every nigga either had too many baby mommas or was broke. I wasn't feeling nobody. I had been partying in D.C. and New York a lot too. The vibe was always good in D.C. I used to go out there a lot back when I was dealing with Mal. He loved D.C. and the club owners there loved him too. He would buy so many bottles. I was able to maintain a few of his relationships, so I could get into most of the clubs for free, and some promoters even would give me free bottles. I was turning into a little socialite and loving every minute of it.

In my travels I was meeting guys, and it was so easy getting shit from out-of-town dudes. I'd tell them anything. I would tell them I owned a business. I was married but just got a divorce. All types of bullshit. They believed anything and cut a nice check. The best part of all was they never pressed me for sex. It was sweet. The new OT guys were helping me pay my bills and keeping me on my feet. I was proud of myself for a change. I didn't feel like I was losing control. I had the upper hand again. Sex wasn't even on my mind.

November

Checking my Instagram notifications, I saw a comment from a page with no profile picture. I went to the page, and it hardly had any photos uploaded. So, I asked who it was. They had to know me in real life based on the things they were writing under my pictures. Finally, they responded and told me to meet them at 7pm on the block. I asked what block, and they said 48th Street. Immediately, I knew who it was. It was Kwan!

I'd met Kwan a few years back. Aaliyah was dating one of his friends, TJ. I would ride through the block with her, and he always walked over to the car to try to talk to me. At the time I was running back and forth over L.A. I was messing with so many guys that I didn't even want to talk to him. Plus, Aaliyah told me he had a lot of kids, and I wasn't trying to be nobody's step-mom. He was also Muslim and very involved with the Muslim community. What did I look like? Dating some serious Muslim? He wasn't about to have me all covered up. I rejected him every single time.

One-night Aaliyah and I went to dinner at Philips, this seafood spot in downtown Philly. We were having a good time when suddenly Kwan walked in, sat next to me, and pleaded his case yet again. I asked him how many kids he had. He said seven.

"Seven kids?" I was in shock. I said, "Well how you gone take care of me plus seven kids?"

He said, "Don't worry. I can handle it, trust me."

We had a long good conversation and before our dinner came to the table he got up and left. He convinced me to give him my number. We ate dinner and waited for the waiter to bring the check, but it never came. I called for the manager because it seemed like the waiter was ignoring us. The manager walked over and asked what the problem was.

"We never got our check." I was clearly annoyed.

"The gentleman paid it," the manager explained.

I was surprised and very apologetic. I was also very impressed. Kwan was smooth and appropriate, and I figured it wouldn't hurt to give him a chance.

Needless to say, I called him the next day and it was on!

Kwan told me he was married to two women at the same time. He was Muslim, and that was allowed in his religion. He had three kids by each wife and an older daughter from a prior relationship. That made me feel a little better about the seven kids' part. Besides him having a ton of kids, Kwan was a good guy. He was the type of guy that didn't have to say much. He had a powerful presence, and everybody respected him. He was a hard worker. He was into real-estate and had a few businesses. I don't know if he was in the streets or not because Kwan would never talk about his business in front of me. We hit it off quick. Kwan loved coffee. I would meet him in the morning at Dunkin Donuts. Once we got close, I would go get his coffee for him: extra-large, extra cream and sugar. That was his shit. Before long, I was staying at his apartment, cooking him food, and even watching his kids. I would even wear an over-garment and cover my hair when he had company in the house. I did it out of respect for Kwan. He never pressured me about becoming Muslim, but he did talk about it a few times. I wasn't doing it unless we were married. He knew I wasn't trying to hear that shit. After like eight months I was falling in love.

He made me feel so special, always buying me stuff and taking me out. And the best part about him was he was a little shy in bed.

I could tell from our first encounter that Kwan wasn't ready for my freaky side. So, I went easy on him. I would pull his dick out and start sucking it at random times, even in the car. He would come in from working all day, and I would jump in the shower with him, wash his back, and suck his dick in the shower. We would be laying in the bed, and I would jump on top, ride him slow until he would cum. Kwan loved for me to control the sex, and I loved it too. He was perfect for me.

One afternoon I got a call from one of his friends, and he told me Kwan was locked up! I couldn't believe it. What could he be locked up for?

I never got an answer, and he never reached out to me while he was in jail. It was like "we" never happened. It was over just like that.

I pulled up on the block and there he was. Kwan was so sexy to me. Tall, light brown skin, he always looked like he had a tan. His beard was always well groomed, and he dressed well. He was wearing some designer jeans and a fitted tee shirt. He had on a very nice jacket, brown suede with a full collar. *Damn*, I was getting flashbacks at the sight of him. I honked the horn to get his attention, and he walked over and climbed into the car. We sat in the car and talked for hours. I told him all the shit I had been through. He told me he had been home for about a year and spending most of his time getting his life back in order. He was fighting for full custody of three of his kids. He was having a rough time. We ended up taking a ride to Southwest Philly. He wanted to show me this daycare he was about to open. Kwan always had a business plan. He knew how to make money. I told him it was a great idea. A lot of people in Philly were making good money in the childcare industry.

Within days we were back on like no time had passed. I couldn't wait to tell Aaliyah that me and Kwan were back together. I called and texted her 100 times. She finally called back and said I was hype, but she knew how I felt about him.

By the end of the week I was meeting him with his coffee at the daycare. We would go out to eat and talk on the phone for hours. He was living in this loft down Northern Liberties, and by the end of the month I had a key. He was still very secretive. He never told me what we went to jail for, and I couldn't tell what he was involved in that was affording him this luxe lifestyle.

Our first time fucking again was so good. Kwan was running around all day, so as soon as we got in the door, he went into the master bathroom to shower. I didn't want to bother him, so I went down the hall and showered in the other bathroom. I didn't take a towel with me, and as I got out the shower I walked towards the bedroom dripping wet. The water created small puddles all over the hardwood floors. Kwan was already in his boxers and a fresh tee-shirt by the time I made it to the bedroom, he was sitting on the side of the bed. I walked in wet, nipples standing straight up. He looked me up and down and smiled. I told him to lay back on the bed. I approached him and pulled his boxers down. Slowly, I kissed his chest, stopped at his belly button and made circles with my tongue, and made my way to the head of his dick. I sucked it slow, popping the head in and out my mouth allowing it to make a loud sound. My mouth got more and more wet. I started to push his entire dick down my throat and making myself gag, allowing more saliva to come running from my mouth. Kwan couldn't take it. His body started to tense up. I stopped and laid my wet body on top of his. My plan was to get on top, but Kwan took control. He flipped me onto the bed and started to suck on my nipples, giving each more attention as my pussy was starting to drip. He took his right hand and plucked my clit just enough to get my juices to flow. He used his left hand to grab my neck and laced himself inside me. It felt like a ton of bricks as he thrusted and pounded his thick dick inside me. This had ever happened before. Kwan was showing off. Ten minutes into it my legs started to shake, and I was cumming. Kwan was still inside me as he whispered in my ear how much he missed me and how good my pussy was. Hearing those words made us both submit. We came together and laid in each other's arms until we fell asleep.

December came and went. Kwan gave me some cash for Christmas even though he didn't celebrate it. I was enjoying being back in his company. The daycare center was almost ready to open too. I was happy for him. He had worked so hard on it. The custody case was leaning in his favor. Seeing him sad about not being with his kids broke my heart. Kwan was an amazing dad he loved his kids, and I know it was hard having to be without them. To plan for the kids to live with him, he brought a new house, a "family house" as he called it. It still needed some work, so Kwan was running nonstop between the daycare and the new house. He wanted both to be perfect. Unless he was working, we were spending almost every night together at the loft. I even let Nia come over a few times. She was still married so she would sneak out and change into "regular" clothes every now and then so she could hang out with me.

Things were good. I had my man back. I was having good sex. He was buying me gifts. I was living a drama free life. My friends and family were noticing a difference in me too. I don't know what it was about Kwan, but I knew I loved him and he loved me too. Just hearing his voice made me smile.

He had my heart, and that's something I couldn't say about no other man I had ever dealt with.

I couldn't wait for the new house to be finished. That's all Kwan talked about, plus he was spending so much time getting it together we weren't able to be together that much. Especially at night. I took him his coffee one morning, and we made plans for the next day. He told me he would call me in the morning, so we could plan a date. He was missing me too. I went on with my day, excited about the quality time we would have very soon. I woke up the next morning and called his phone. No answer. I texted him, waited a few hours, but no response. So, I went back to sleep. Maybe he worked all night and was still sleep? Kwan was a morning person, so I figured that had to be the case. I jumped up when I heard my phone ringing. It was Aaliyah.

"You talk to Kwan?" she asked.

"Not since last night," I said. "We are getting together later today, though. Why, what's up?"

She got quiet.

"Aaliyah, what's up?" I can tell she's hiding something.

"I'm so sorry," she kept repeating. "I'm so sorry!" I could tell she was crying.

"What? What's going on?"

"TJ just called me and told me Kwan got shot last night, and he didn't make it."

My head started spinning. I hung up the phone on her and dialed TJ's number, but he didn't answer. I called and texted Kwan like fifteen times. This shit had to be a lie. I was just with him. We were back together. We had a date that day!

TJ finally called me back and confirmed what Aaliyah told me. I broke down. My heart was pounding. I couldn't breathe.

Shit felt like a nightmare, I think I sat in the same spot for hours. I replayed the last few months in my mind repeatedly. No Kwan wasn't the first man I dated that got killed, but this time hurt more then before. I mean we had made plans, It felt like love. I went from being sad to feeling stupid. It would never be that easy for me, I mean who was I kidding? I didn't have much time to grieve Kwan was Muslim so he had to be buried within 48 hours. Aaliyah and I attended his Janazah (Muslim funeral). I walked into the funeral home in slow motion. It was packed with so many people that loved and respected Kwan. The Muslim community in Philadelphia was very large, so I knew it was going to be crowded. I approached his casket and looked at his face for the last time. He looked so peaceful. I rushed out the door, so no one would see the tears rolling down my face. Aaliyah left, and I sat in my car and cried my eyes out. I didn't want to stay for the whole service. It was happening too fast. I was just with him just lying in the bed beside him less than a week ago. I couldn't stop thinking about his kids, and how their lives would never be the same. Kwan was such a great father. My heart ached for them.

The next few weeks were horrible. I was going through the motions. One minute I was fine and next thing you know I would be in bed for days crying. I didn't understand why this was happening to me. I thought Kwan coming back in my life was a sign from God. I wanted that to be my happy ending. We could have been so much more. He made me smile, and he didn't care about my past or who I had been with before him. He was so special to me, and now he was gone.

I vowed that I wouldn't have sex again until I was in a serious relationship. I had to set some boundaries. I wanted to be in love again. I was no longer interested in controlling a man with my pussy or taking money and gifts to make up for lack of commitment. I was ready for the real thing. I wanted to mean something to somebody.

As much as I wanted to be in a relationship I was scared. I didn't want to feel the pain of losing someone I loved again, so I told myself no more street guys. That's all there seemed to be in Philly, though. Either they were in the streets or once were. I didn't have time for no more fed cases. So, I swore off men entirely.

I was over it.

I was done!

Summer 1998

My best friend Crystal finally got her new car. We had been sneaking and using her mom's car, but we always had to be back home early so we wouldn't get caught. She was so excited to have a car of her own, a cherry red convertible! People always thought we were sisters. We looked so much alike: tall, the same complexion, and we even wore the same size clothes and shoes. Crystal was about two years older than me, but it didn't matter because I was way more mature than my age.

We put the new car on the road right away. We drove to New York to party at this gay club. We weren't trying to meet anyone. We just liked to dance, and we would be so tired driving home from the city we had to find somewhere closer to go. Somebody told us about this spot in Philly that had the same vibe, so we started going there instead. We would go every Friday night. It was so much fun, and they played the best music. We had fake IDs, so we would drink tequila sunrises and party all night long. After a few weeks we were considered "regulars," so they stopped carding us. We would get approached by women too. At first they thought we were a couple, Crystal and I would crack up laughing. We told everybody we were sisters. That news spread like a wildfire, and the date requests started pouring in. Crystal started embracing the whole lesbian thing before I did. At first, I thought it was cute having a bunch of older chicks chasing us around the club and buying us drinks. But I realized they really were gay, and I didn't want to play with anyone's feelings. I would reject the offers. Crystal started going on dates, and by the end of summer she was damn near in a whole relationship.

By the fall it was hard not to find some of the women attractive. I mean lesbians came in all different shapes and sizes. There were boyish ones with great bodies. Feminine ones like me and Crystal that wore dresses and sexy heels. There were some that didn't wear girly clothes but still had girly hair styles. They were called "soft butch." Those were my favorite type of females. They had the hard side like a guy but were still pretty like a girl. My cousin had started hanging in the club with us too. She was coming out of the closet slowly, so she was happy when we brought her out the first time. I could tell she felt like she could be herself. We had our little crew. Everybody knew us, and we knew all the right people too.

I finally gave in and started dating this girl Gina. She was a soft butch, light brown skin, about 5'8" with an athletic build. She always bought me drinks in the club and asked me on dates. I always ignored her before, but one night as I was leaving the bathroom, she backed me into the corner and kissed me! Her lips were so soft. I was shocked, but it felt so good. I agreed to go out with her, and we hit it off instantly from there. I never thought about girls in a romantic way, but Gina had a way of making me forget she was a girl. We spent so much time together. Her friends and my friends became cool. We formed a little click and went to the club together every weekend.

Our sexual connection was more intense than our emotional one. Gina knew what to do to make me feel good. She would touch me and my body would get warm. She didn't ever want me to touch her. I would beg to suck on her nipples, and sometimes she would let me. She preferred to lay between my legs and feast on my pussy for hours. I would feel myself releasing in her mouth repeatedly. We would lay up in her apartment all day long, naked in bed.

Dating Gina wasn't all good though. She had a lot of drama. Her ex-girlfriend was this older chick from "down the bottom," this small section of West Philly. Chicks from down there were known for fighting! She was no different. She hated the idea of me and Gina being together. She tried to make my life a living hell. She would come to the club and bump me, and she would talk shit about me to anybody that listened. We got in a huge fight outside a bar once. It was bad. She ended up busting my bedroom window out, and that's when I knew it was going too far. Gina tried to help me and calm the tension, but this girl was crazy. In the end, I didn't feel like it was worth it to get hurt for some pussy. Plus, I wasn't gay. The shit was fun, but I wasn't trying to marry a chick.

I dated a few more females throughout my teens. I had one other serious relationship with a chick I met in the club. Her name was Erica. Erica was a little older than me. She had a son, and she was still in a relationship with her son's father. He was a rich Spanish drug lord from North Philly. Erica was very pretty and feminine like me. We could have passed for sisters. From the first day I met her she treated me like a goddess. She bought me expensive gifts on an almost a daily basis. I would spend the night at her house and sleep in the bed with her and her son's dad. We told him I was her long-lost cousin. He believed her, so that made it easy for us to spend a lot of time together. They shared a cute two-bedroom apartment in the northeast section of Philly. He barely knew English, and he was even worse at counting money. Erica would oversee the counting his money after he made drops to the people he supplied drugs for in the city. I would help her count the money sometimes. Sometimes it would be thousands of dollars a day. Since he wasn't very smart, we were able to steal tons of money from him. Erica would hide the money we took in the pots and pans and sometimes even in the cereal boxes. We would wake up and count our stash, never knowing how much we had taken the night before. Erica and I had a very sensual connection. Sex with her was very emotional, unlike any of my other experiences. She also didn't like me to perform sexual acts on her. She allowed me to be the one to experience pleasure, and that's what I did. Our connection was special. I secretly always knew Erica and I wouldn't last long. Her son's father was the bread winner. She needed him, and it was clear that I could never be the provider she was used to. So after about two years, I just stopped. It was like we never were.

Females were very emotional. Everything was about feelings, and I found relationships with women to be very intense. I was way too young to be involved with something so deep.

Crystal continued to date girls, and I continued to only have sex with them.

As we got older, Crystal and I stopped hanging out together as much. We were in two different places. I would come out to big Gay Pride events and any time Crystal needed me to be her sidekick I would go out with her.

By the time I graduated high school I classified myself as bisexual, not knowing my attraction to the same sex would haunt me for the rest of my life...

Fall 2016

No sex in almost three years. No threesomes, no Bee, no crazy episodes, no Nia either. She was a totally different person. I felt like I didn't even know who she was anymore. She had some struggles with her mental health. I tried to there for her, but she would have episodes that caused her to be placed in facilities. By the time she was released, her phone would be cut off. She would text me from new numbers a few times a year. So when I didn't her from her, I knew that meant she was hospitalized. It really broke my heart to see Nia going through her struggles. I mean, she was one of my favorite people in the world. We were so close, and watching her personality slip away and her beauty fade was horrible. I wanted the best for her. I wanted my friend back.

I had adopted this no new friend's mentality. I was not interested in getting to know nobody else. I had my core circle of friends. A lot of us were into different things, so we didn't get to hang out a lot, but I knew who to call and when.

I was pretty much alone. And I was ok with that.

Winter

Why was it so hard for me to cut ties with men from my past?

After damn near five years, Industry hit me up. He said he just wanted to see how I was doing. His voice still sounded the same; his tone and the way he spoke was so sexy. I drifted off into a fantasy world thinking about how things would be if he and I were back together. I began to visualize the way he used to fuck me, the look in his eyes when I used to suck on his nipples. He was the first man to get me to loosen up. Just the sound of his voice brought back so many freaky memories. We had so much chemistry. So many years had passed. I thought I would be over him, but my reaction to hearing him say my name on the other end of the phone was proof that he still had me. He still owned a piece of me. I couldn't understand how. I mean, I was so much older now, and I owned my power!

Industry wanted to know every single detail about the last five years of my life. I wasn't sharing too much, but I told him I was single, and that sex wasn't a huge part of my life anymore. He wasn't trying to hear that. He laughed at me and insisted that I must have been dealing with a bunch of lames because I had some of the best sex in the world (his words). He asked me if I remembered the last time we had sex. I said I didn't, but I did. We were in L.A. We showered together and fucked for hours. He was so good in bed there was no way I could forget that.

He did a good job of providing some of the best sexual memories for me, and after all this time I could still remember the first time we fucked, how good he felt inside me, and how tight my pussy held on to this dick while it was inside me. I could picture doing it just one more time. He told me he had relocated to Miami and was thinking about moving to Atlanta by the end of the year. He was still doing music and managing a few artists. He said he missed me so much. After the first time we talked, he started calling me damn near every day.

At first it was innocent conversations, but it quickly escalated into phone sex. Really good phone sex. So good I went out and brought a new toy, a G-spot Rabbit. It was hot pink with an extra piece on it that sat right on the clitoris. He would dominate me by telling me how fast or slow to run the vibrator. I would lay in my bed and squirt uncontrollably. He had me stuck. I looked forward to seeing his number pop up on my screen. I was able to release some much-needed stress and hearing him tell me how beautiful I was made our interaction so much more of a necessity. The sexual chemistry between us was intense, but I felt so stupid. Here I was five years later being a fool for a man that would never be mine. I wanted to cut him off, but my body was telling me no.

Weeks went by and I started to feel myself slipping back to a place I wasn't ready to go. I woke up one morning to some graphic text from Industry. He always had a way with words. I almost texted him back, but instead I deleted his number. I deleted the whole thread. I get out of bed, showered, and went on about my day. By the end of the day, he had called me a ton of times and texted to see if I was alright. I was. I just refused to respond. He got irked after a few days and called me all types of names. Typical behavior. He couldn't get what he wanted, so it was fuck me. I was quickly reminded of why we didn't work out all those years ago. His temper was fucked up. He just wanted to mind fuck me and have me as his sex puppet. Nothing had changed with him, and I couldn't go backwards. I had done so much work on myself. I was no longer craving the control. I didn't want to be a sex object. Before he hit me up, I wasn't even thinking about sex.

Industry was a test and I failed. This was the moment I decided it was time for a change.

Penetration is my story. Raw, real, and unapologetic.
Thank you for taking this journey with me.
This is only the beginning.

Sheena E.

Vol. 2

LOVE over LUST

Made in the USA
Middletown, DE
17 February 2019